# OUR HOUSE
# DIVIDED

# OUR HOUSE
# DIVIDED

## Seven Japanese American
## Families in World War II

### Tomi Kaizawa Knaefler

A KOLOWALU BOOK

University of Hawaii Press

Honolulu

92 93 94 95  5 4 3 2

**Library of Congress Cataloging-in-Publication Data**

Knaefler, Tomi Kaizawa, 1929–
Our house divided : seven Japanese American families
in World War II / Tomi Kaizawa Knaefler.
p.    cm. — (A Kolowalu book)
Includes bibliographical references and index.
ISBN 0–8248–1045–7
1.  World War, 1939–1945—Japanese Americans.
2.  World War, 1939–1945—Hawaii.   3.  Japanese
Americans—Hawaii—History—20th century.   4.   World War,
1939–1945—Participation, Japanese-American.
5.  Hawaii—History—1900–1959.   I.   Title.
D753.8K57   1991
996.9'004956—dc20                91–19279
CIP

University of Hawaii Press books are
printed on acid-free paper and meet the
guidelines for permanence and durability
of the Council on Library Resources

*Book design by Paula Newcomb*

*To my daughter, Pamela, my son, Jim,
my ex-husband Jim, my Kaizawa family,
and my* Honolulu Star-Bulletin
*and* Honolulu Advertiser *colleagues*

# Contents

# Foreword

The origin of this book goes back to the fall of 1966 in the news room of the *Honolulu Star-Bulletin* when Tomi Knaefler was a reporter and I was the managing editor. The twenty-fifth anniversary of Japan's December 7, 1941, attack on Pearl Harbor that plunged the United States into World War II was fast approaching, and we who were then editors were brainstorming for a centerpiece to commemorate the day in more than perfunctory fashion.

My own thoughts flashed back to southern Pennsylvania, where I had grown up near Gettysburg, the northernmost point of penetration by the armies of the Confederacy in the American Civil War of 1861–1865. I had often walked the grounds where Pickett's Southerners once had charged into the rifle and cannon fire of Union defenders to be decimated in the turning-point battle of the war.

What fascinated me most then, as now, was that the men on opposite sides of that bloody war were often friends, even brothers, drawn by complex forces into fighting as foes despite all their love of each other personally. It seemed, and still seems, especially poignant, especially cruel, especially illuminating of the tragedy that war is.

I naively thought that the occurrence of brother fighting against brother was something out of the past. Even when World War II came along I still thought so. My ancestry is German but my forebears had been in America for two centuries. I had no kin fighting on the other side and didn't know anyone who did.

It was only after I moved to Hawaii in 1946, following service in the U.S. Navy in the Pacific, that I learned that the agony of families divided, of brother fighting brother, had been replicated, perhaps even more tragically than at Gettysburg, in the Pacific War between the United States and Japan. Over 37 percent of the population in Hawaii at the time of Pearl Harbor was comprised of people who either had been born in Japan or were only one generation removed. The largest single source of these Japanese immigrants had been Hiroshima Prefecture.

Here, then, was a story about the Pacific War that had not yet been told—a story of divided loyalties perhaps even greater in magnitude than those occurring during the Civil War or during any other conflict in which this phenomenon, the result of population movement, has occurred.

On our staff there was no one who could remotely approach Tomi Knaefler's qualifications to do such a story. The war was still a sensitive issue, so the task would be to seek out these families and to gain their cooperation in discussing their innermost feelings. Tomi was of Japanese ancestry herself. Her parents had come from Hiroshima Prefecture. She was the *Star-Bulletin*'s first full-time woman reporter of Japanese ancestry. She was the hardest-digging reporter any editor could hope to have on his staff. Her great strength was her fierce determination to learn everything about any story she was assigned to. She was always particularly anxious to understand the human side of a news story, not in a sensationalizing sob-sister fashion, but out of a determined need to know why people did what they did, and how they felt about it. She had a way of asking the most personal questions with such sincerity and genuine caring that they did not seem offensive. She had a track record for impeccable accuracy as a reporter. Hardly ever did anyone say she was wrong in what she wrote. But more than once people had said that they had told her more than they had intended to.

When the "House Divided" series was completed, my spine

tingled as I read some of the stories. They were so real, so often painfully vivid. Now, twenty-five years later, I still get that reaction.

I felt in 1966 that "House Divided" deserved the permanence of a book as opposed to the transitory nature of a newspaper series, which is read and then discarded. But in 1966, American book publishers informed us that the subject matter was much too sensitive. I am glad that the University of Hawaii Press is now publishing this book in time for the fiftieth anniversary of Pearl Harbor. Even now it is still a little-told story.

For years to come, it will offer insight into an important episode in the building of Hawaii and America. That I had a hand in its creation is a source of great pride.

A. A. (Bud) Smyser
Contributing Editor
*Honolulu Star-Bulletin*
Honolulu, Hawaii

# INTRODUCTION

This book begins with the bombing of Pearl Harbor on December 7, 1941. It tells the stories of seven Japanese American families of Hawaii that were split geographically and emotionally between Japan and the United States by World War II. The stories, based on interviews I conducted in 1966 as a newspaper reporter for the *Honolulu Star-Bulletin,* were published to commemorate the twenty-fifth anniversary of Pearl Harbor. They now appear in book form on this, the fiftieth anniversary of that day.

Working on this book has been unexpectedly painful for me. I was jolted into realizing that their story—the story of these seven families of *Our House Divided*—was also my story. My family, too, had been divided by World War II. This realization led me on a disquieting inward journey during which I saw how the wartime hatred and distrust unleashed in the United States against Japanese Americans coupled with my vulnerability at age 12 had profoundly affected me. I discovered that I had felt guilty about Pearl Harbor and had carried that burden around for well over forty years. I also realized that I had begun to deny my Japaneseness, my very roots, because the Japanese were the "bad guys" and it hurt too much to be Japanese.

As it was for those I interviewed for *Our House Divided,* the internal conflict created by the war was also intensely painful for me—so much so that I suppressed the experience. It wasn't until a late afternoon in November of 1983, while visiting the Munch-Museet in Oslo, Norway, that the buried childhood pain returned to me. I was moving leisurely through the main gallery of the museum, absorbed in Edvard Munch's soul-stirring paintings of toiling Norwegian villagers. When I found myself facing his masterpiece, *The Scream,* I was sucked into the contorted face of the screamer. My head, or was it my chest, felt as if it would burst. I rushed outside. The tears flowed as I walked in the soft Norwegian snow. The painting had triggered a flashback of the soundless screams that had overwhelmed me on a November day in 1941 when my ailing father left Hawaii for Japan and then again a month later when Japan bombed Pearl Harbor—the two events that conspired to divide my family.

Like the families in *Our House Divided,* my family was shocked when war came and at the way it came. The attack on Pearl Harbor and adjacent military installations on Hawaii's most populated island, Oahu, occurred at 7:55 A.M., but it was not until midday that word reached our remote sugar plantation village of Pahoa on Hawaii, the southernmost island in the Hawaiian archipelago. I was barely 12. I remember that we had just finished singing, praying, and hearing heaven-and-hell stories at the Young Buddhist Association's meeting hall. My friends and I were playing in the neighborhood park when we heard the urgent Clang! Clang! Clang! of the plantation's old alarm, which usually sounded when shifting winds whipped a cane harvest fire out of control. We searched the sky for the telltale black smoke, but there was none.

We ran to the Buddhist meeting hall and saw a plantation supervisor frantically striking the metal alarm and yelling: "Attack! Attack! Japan bombed Pearl Harbor. Lot of people dead."

Like the people in this book, I did not know what to think. I only knew this was a terrible thing. I was frightened. My friends looked scared too. As we scattered for our homes, I felt even more frightened, thinking about my father and grandfather, whom we had not heard from since they had sailed out of Honolulu Harbor for Japan thirty-two days earlier aboard the *Taiyo maru.*

The author, *right,* at age 12 and her friend Alice Shiigi (now Chinen) walking to school along Pahoa's main street. *Author's photo collection.*

My father had come from Hiroshima Prefecture in 1898 to work for the sugar plantations in Hawaii. Then he had been full of cocky vigor and adventurous spirit at age 22. He returned home to Hiroshima a multiple stroke victim of 65 in a wheelchair with severely impaired speech and paralysis throughout his left side. He was going home, fulfilling a wish commonly held by the older Japanese of that period, to spend their last days in their homeland. My father was accompanied by my maternal grandfather, a jaunty fisherman of 69. Since 1899 my grandfather ("Jit-chan") had lived part of the time in the family home in Hiroshima with my grandmother and had spent the rest of the time sampan fishing out of Hilo on the island of Hawaii (the Big Island).

As I neared my house, I saw neighbors huddled in front of our hibiscus hedge talking with my mother. They looked tense and worried. A few doors from our house, Mrs. Moniz had her radio blaring and I heard a man's voice say, "Yellow Japs." The words stunned me. In that instant I realized that everything had changed. Japan, which had been such a strong influence on my life, was now the enemy. I churned with anger and shame that a nation of people related to me had done something so horrible. I thought about a lesson etched in my mind at an early age— that whatever I did, good or bad, would reflect upon my family, my community, and the Japanese race as a whole. So why did the Japanese do this to me, to all of us? I felt betrayed.

I didn't express my feelings to anyone. Ours was a traditional Japanese family. We were taught by example to be stoic, not to express our feelings, and not to burden others. I found this same pattern of Japanese restraint in the families I interviewed for *Our House Divided.*

My mother did talk to us about the unlikelihood of hearing from my father and grandfather as long as the war continued. After that initial talk, I don't recall that we ever mentioned them again until the war ended, even though I am sure they were always in our thoughts. In our Japanese community, we were the only family divided in that way by the war, although most, if not all, of the issei (first generation immigrants) had close relatives in Japan. Like my mother they found comfort during the war in their daily Buddhist ritual of prayers and offerings before the family shrine. But I remember them being shocked and nervous on December 7, 1941.

There was cause for more uneasiness later that day when a neighbor, Mrs. Mukai, told my mother that the Filipinos in the community, enraged over Japan's bombing of Manila that same morning, were sharpening their cane knives. I remember the terror in my 10-year-old brother Carl's eyes. My mother swiftly hushed such talk as nonsense. Mrs. Mukai also said that the Buddhist temples and Japanese language schools throughout Hawaii were to be closed. My mother could not speak for a moment. Then she asked, "What will happen to the children?"

The language school was an important part of our village life. All Japanese children went there after regular public school to learn not only the language but Japanese values, etiquette, and culture. Ironically, my old classmate Yoshito Miyatake recalled that his favorite subject in language school was learning about Lincoln, Washington, and other heroes. The school was a tremendous help to the mothers, most of whom worked from sunrise to sunset in the canefields alongside the men.

What distressed my mother most of all was that Mr. Izuno, our Japanese school principal, the Buddhist priests, and two Japanese community leaders had been taken into custody by the FBI.

(Four of the issei in *Our House Divided* were similarly arrested. They were among the 1,441 Japanese in Hawaii whom the FBI initially picked up for internment, although the actual number interned for the duration of the war was 980. Half of them were *kibei,* young American-born Japanese who received some or all of their schooling in Japan and then returned to the United States.)

I was shaken by the FBI arrests too. Did this mean that strict and solemn Mr. Izuno was a dangerous criminal or spy? And what about the Buddhist priests who chanted in sing-song as they burned incense and bonged on the temple bells? Were they dangerous, too? I wanted to ask my mother, but I did not want to upset her further.

I was even more shaken when I first learned of the mass evacuation of some 120,000 Japanese alien residents and U.S. citizens from the West Coast. I could not imagine what that entailed. Books such as *Farewell to Manzanar* and *Personal Justice Denied,* which I read in the 1980s, and film documentaries I saw later enabled me to grasp what had taken place. Pressure for a similar evacuation of Hawaii's Japanese was exerted from Washington, but cooler heads prevailed among Hawaii's military and civilian leadership, and only about a thousand Islanders, mostly dependents of those already interned, were evacuated to mainland camps. For one thing, the leadership was aware that a mass evacuation would spell economic disaster. In 1941 there were 160,000 Japanese in Hawaii, which was over 37 percent of the total population of 423,000. What I remember of the evacuation is that two of my classmates were there one day and gone the next—swallowed up by something called "the war."

However frightening and ugly December 7 had been, my most indelible memory of the day was of my mother and our Portuguese neighbor, Isabelle Perreira, standing on the path between our houses, hugging each other and sobbing as they reaffirmed their bond of friendship of thirty years. The two women had arrived in Pahoa as young brides and had shared their ups and downs as they adjusted to their new lives and raised their children in this raw, new plantation village.

"You and me sisters no matter what," Mrs. Perreira said. My mother nodded, "Yes."

As it was for the *Our House Divided* families, the first impact of war was so powerful for me, I had no time to think as we plunged into wartime. For a 12-year-old in the middle of Pahoa's canefields, there was no denying that it was exciting, with something new happening all the time. First came martial law, which remained in effect until October 1944, and strict blackout and curfew regulations that were not eased until mid-1943 and finally lifted in May 1944. Fingerprinting also occurred, as well as typhoid and smallpox shots, blood-typing, air raid and gas mask drills, and the planting of sweet potato gardens in the event of a rice shortage. Then came some two hundred GIs in truckloads. I never dreamed there were so many haoles (caucasians). It was like a Cecil B. DeMille production. A plump, red-headed teacher, our town's first from the mainland, was so overjoyed to see the soldiers she flung open her classroom windows and, with her floppy hat bobbing up and down, led the entire student body in singing "Over There," "Yankee Doodle Dandy," "Anchors Aweigh," and the like, while the GIs hollered and cheered.

Overnight, Pahoa jumped to life to respond to the recreational needs of the soldiers. Two bars sprang up. Jukeboxes appeared. The Akebono Theater showed movies every night. Our main street with no name was jammed every evening with hard-smoking, fast-talking GIs, cocky in their well-creased uniforms. For the villagers, it was an eye-opener to see so many caucasians who weren't plantation bosses.

On Sundays our school park turned into a major baseball diamond for the troops, and in the afternoon the USO staged a hula show with beautiful blonde dancers in their glittering Dorothy Lamour cellophane skirts with matching bras. The dancers were from the main town of Hilo and were not the authentic Hawaiian dancers from neighboring Kalapana. The soldiers loved it. So did my friends and I. We had never seen anything so glamorous.

For my sister Ellen and her high school chums, the big weekly event was the Saturday night USO dance in the school gym with a GI orchestra playing the big band sounds. Ellen could go because our neighbor, Mrs. Perreira, was one of the chaperones. My sister and her friends could hardly wait to hear the latest Hit Parade songs and to learn new dance steps from the "cute" GIs. I was too young to go. So my neighbor Dolores and I were content baking tomato juice cakes with butter icing for the dances. Our reward was hearing how quickly our cakes were devoured. Also for the war effort, I made a blue-and-white skirt with "God Bless America" sewn at the hemline in red rick-rack.

Once, my friends and I peeked in at the USO dance, totally unprepared for such exuberance—the faces of the dancers glistening and their backs drenched as they glided, twirled, and jitterbugged in all directions to the overpowering music: "Chattanooga Choo Choo," "Boogie Woogie Bugle Boy," "In the Mood," "Flight of the Bumble Bee," and so on. We stood in the doorway gawking until Mrs. Perreira shooed us home.

The townspeople seemed to enjoy the excitement brought by the GIs, except for the local fellows, who felt jealous when the girls started to attend the dances. My sister and her friends talked about some "dirty looks" they got as they walked in a group to the gym all gussied up and obviously excited.

Unlike the severe food shortages in Japan so vividly recalled by those I interviewed for this book, wartime shortages in our village were not a problem because we raised so much of our own food. We did have to wait for shipments of canned and bottled goods, flour, rice, and Washington apples. The gas shortage was not a problem because most families did not own cars, and the shortage of shoes and clothing was not a hardship for people like my mother who were habitually resourceful.

But there were some things I did miss, like the summer *obon* dances the Japanese traditionally held to honor the dead, and Japanese Boys' Day and Girls' Day festivities, all of which were now banned. I also missed cracked plum seed, a spicy sweet-sour preserve from China that remains a favorite treat for Island children. Throughout the war I made my own cracked seed with dried prunes marinated in a chutney-like sauce of lemon juice, cider vinegar, raw sugar, and salt. I also yearned to have the blackout lifted so that I could see the stars through my open window, smell the sweet country air, and feel the wind blowing through the white curtains. I soon learned to create my own open window in my mind.

As the months went by the edge of the wartime excitement wore off. The novelty of carrying the gas mask quickly palled. The bulky device became a burden, like lugging around a leg of lamb in a canvas bag strapped across my chest. Pahoa, a typical island plantation village, went about its usual business. Or so it seemed to me.

It was only as I began to conduct research for this book that I became aware of just how confused and frightened the normally well-ordered adult Japanese community must have been as it was stripped of its leaders, temples, and traditions. Tim Klass, author of *World War II on Kauai,* has observed that the issei were so fearful and demoralized that they were reluctant to take on any leadership positions for fear they would be interned. He said they had no choice but to accept the dismantling of every institution that had held Hawaii's Japanese community together.

Among the most important of these institutions were the Buddhist temples, according to University of Hawaii sociologist Andrew W. Lind. In his book *Hawaii's Japanese,* Lind says that the shutdown of the temples created a "religious vacuum" which Christian sects could not really fill. He says the most damaging thing suffered by the issei was a "sudden forfeiture of respect and authority in the eyes of their own children," which, he writes, was "one of the most cruel by-products of the war."

Regulations also made the issei feel trapped and vulnerable, such as security restrictions on travel and on change of residence or occupation without a permit. Only English was permitted on the telephone and in letters. Most issei were unable to communicate in English.

I also learned from my research that the five Japanese Americans who were nominated in Hawaii's election primaries in 1942 were pressured to withdraw. Even the *New York Daily News* got into the act: "It seems inescapable that we have got to exercise some old style imperialism in Hawaii for the duration of the war to be on the safe side. We cannot afford the risk of having any apple carts upset in those islands by the present or former subjects of the Mikado, and if the Japanese in Hawaii don't like that attitude they had better go back where they or their ancestors came from." When the candidates withdrew, they were praised for their patriotism by Hawaii's Governor Ingram M. Stainback.

At 12, I was unaware of such goings on. Because the Japanese adults around me were so typically stoic and protective, I didn't hear of their frustration and fear. Instead, the message I got was that everything was okay, that we had to accept things like the closing of the Buddhist temples and the internment of community leaders as part of war. *Shikata ga nai* (Can't help it. What must be, must be).

My mother, like the people I interviewed, accepted the assorted bans and restrictions without a word. But I could tell that the order against wearing kimonos in public made her sad. The art of the kimono had always given her such pleasure. Once or twice each year women of our community gathered at our home to view bolt after bolt of the latest silks imported from Japan by a merchant in Hilo. The women were all atwitter as they fingered the silks and draped them over their shoulders in front of the mirror. They giggled and chirped—a group of women at a hen party. My mother's eyes sparkled as she helped the women make their selections in a sea of lavish color. Later, she sewed the kimonos, and at the next festive occasion, the women were decked out in style.

I had often shared in my mother's joy in the kimono world. When she sat on the cushioned floor in the evening to sew the garments after her day's work was done, I would sit next to her and sew my doll's clothes or rummage through her old lacquer sewing chests filled with bright silk threads and geometric patterns for sashes.

My sister Ellen and I helped my mother the day she said goodbye to the kimono tradition. We hung out the stacks of kimonos and thick brocaded sashes called obis, which represented years of loving handicraft, for a last airing in the hot sun. Our clotheslines were a riot of color and design. Then my mother gently folded and wrapped each kimono and obi in cotton covers and placed them into her lacquer *tansu* (chest of drawers) with pieces of camphor tucked into the corners.

The packing ceremony took several hours, and through it all my mother seemed lost in thought, as if she were preparing her kimono children for a long sleep. I remember her sadness. My mother learned later that some families, overwhelmed with fear, had buried or burned their heirloom kimonos, their religious and other symbolic artifacts, and even their family photographs taken in Japan.

I had grown up taking my pride in being Japanese for granted, but now I wondered whether it was so terrible to be Japanese that you had to destroy the evidence. I had no doubt at all about my allegiance to the United States. This was my country. This was my home. Yet, I could not deny my emotional ties to Japan. My father and grandparents, my mother's younger sister whom she adored, and many other relatives were there. I had never even met any of those relatives, but I knew they were important to my mother and I felt a bond.

Until Pearl Harbor, I was happy being a hyphenated Japanese-American. My childhood was country—sugar plantation country of pastureland, secret groves of the sweetest, plumpest guavas and ruby red mountain apples, thimbleberry patches nestled around moss rocks, the tadpole pond, constant rainbows, the weather-beaten post office by our house where people gathered for the noon mail, warm *futon* (thick comforters) we sandwiched ourselves in, our *ofuro* (hot tub), the bookmobile, steaming *udon* (noodles) on cold nights, Best Foods mayonnaise spread on Hilo Saloon Pilot Crackers, our neighbor's fresh Portuguese bread, high heels made of string and empty spools, my mother playing with my hair.

And, waiting each month for my brother Stanley's *Boy's Life* magazine, roller-skating down Catholic Church hill, marching in my short, flared band uniform, trying out my sister Matsuko's bright red lipstick, yanking fresh sugarcane off the train cars, wishing my father wasn't sick.

My father had suffered the first of a series of devastating strokes when my brother Carl and I were still little. The only son of a farming family in Oko town, near Hiroshima City, he came to Hawaii only three weeks after Hawaii was annexed to the United States on the twelfth day in August 1898, when native Hawaiians sadly saw their flag lowered—"fluttering like a wounded bird"*—and replaced by the Stars and Stripes.

My father had been among the 213,750 Japanese immigrants —mostly from southwestern Japan—who made the 4,000-mile journey across the Pacific between 1868 and 1924, before the U.S. Oriental Exclusion Act was passed. The act was aimed at the Japanese in response to continued anti-Japanese agitation in California and to the fear among Hawaii's white elite of a potential political threat from the burgeoning Japanese population. The law stayed in effect until 1952.

Within a couple of years after my father's arrival, the Japanese constituted the largest ethnic group in Hawaii—40 percent out of a total population of 154,000. And they made up 70 percent of the sugar industry's labor force, despite the fact that three-quarters of those who came earlier had returned to Japan or moved to the mainland after completing their contracts.

My family knows very little about my father's earliest years in Hawaii, except that he learned to speak English and Hawaiian and to write English. He worked at the store of Hawaii's first lumber export company, which flourished in Pahoa from 1907 to 1917, supplying *ohia* railroad ties to the Santa Fe Railway in California. He worked as a house painter for the Olaa Sugar Company after the lumber mill folded. Faded photographs show my mother arrived in Hawaii in 1913 at age seventeen, wearing a silk kimono in a subdued pattern with her long, black hair swept up in a full bouffant.

---

*In the words of a bystander, quoted by E. B. Scott, in *The Saga of the Sandwich Islands*. p. 309.

Japanese contract workers arrive at Honolulu dock, c. 1899. *Hawaii State Archives Photo.*

Like most of the *Our House Divided* families, we lived in the same house with the same neighbors in the same community until the children were grown. In our case, there were seven children—four sons and three daughters, born every second or third year, and raised in the same five-room *ohia* wood house.

While my siblings and I don't recall racially related hostility aimed at us before the war, we were aware of the built-in social and economic hierarchy based on race. It was the white men who were the bosses with heavy leather boots and John Wayne hats. They never talked directly to the laborers, only through their Portuguese *lunas* (supervisors), and they lived in grand hilltop houses in a prewar lifestyle that author Klass describes as "baronial."

My siblings and I grew up essentially ignorant about Hawaiian and plantation history. I thought of Hawaii as White

America, not Hawaiian. It was only after reading Lawrence H. Fuchs' *Hawaii Pono* and Gavan Daws' *Shoal of Time* in the 1960s that I became aware of our history and the systemic discrimination against the Asian immigrants. For example, it was Fuchs who first pointed up this prewar paradox: The white leadership wanted the Japanese to speak good English, wear American clothes, play baseball, eat hot dogs, join the Boy Scouts, and become Christians, but heaven forbid that they should ask for equal opportunity.

I believe that had I been aware of the history of racism endured by the Asians in America, I would not have been so stunned by the hate and distrust against the "Japs" that spewed out after December 7, 1941, from the radio, newspapers, comic books, and the movies. I learned from several *Our House Divided* interviews that other nisei shared the same feelings of anger, shame, and guilt that had erupted in me that first day of the war. But at the time, those feelings were my private pain. I didn't know whether my sisters and brothers or friends shared my feelings. Sometimes I thought I could sense the mutual pain in our language of silence. But I was never sure. I wondered whether children whose parents had come from Germany and Italy felt the same way. But they at least looked like white Americans. The Japanese did not. I did not. But more than my appearance, it was the idea of being so hated for being born Japanese that gnawed at me. Even at age 12, or perhaps because of my vulnerable age, I felt an enormous conflict about being Japanese. It hurt so much.

I'll always remember the day I was glancing through a magazine in my dentist's waiting room in Hilo. The words jumped out at me: "Once a Jap always a Jap." They referred to the mass evacuation of the Japanese on the West Coast. I felt terrible. Not even the sight of my dentist smoking a cigar through a baby bottle nipple could make me laugh. I wondered whether that was the way people on the mainland thought. There was no one in Pahoa I could ask.

I knew at the time that nisei (American citizens of issei parents), men like my brother Stanley, were not being accepted for military service even though they were American citizens. It wasn't until much later that I could understand the double bind these nisei men were caught in. Their loyalty was questioned because of their racial origin. The only way they could dispel that distrust was to fight for their country. Yet, military service was denied them, and their loyalty remained under a dark cloud.

The nisei cadet officers and graduates of the University of Hawaii ROTC were not allowed to do guard duty. One of these officers, a friend of mine, later told me, "They needed guards, but they did not want us because they did not trust us. To the powers-that-be we were Japs. It made me feel like a nothing, like a traitor."

But he and his friends persisted. They formed a labor battalion called the Varsity Victory Volunteers to dig ditches, lay roads, and string barbed wire for the Army Corps of Engineers. "That we were allowed to do," he said.

I remember Stanley's impassioned letter sent to my mother soon after Pearl Harbor while he was at the University of Hawaii. He said that volunteering to fight for America was the only way to prove his loyalty and to win equality for the Japanese. He said he had to show America that "if you cut off my arm it will bleed the same as a white man's would." For days the image of Stanley's bleeding arm haunted me.

In *Our House Divided,* several of the nisei describe that same intense frustration and the even more intense will to win the right to fight for their country. Acceptance finally came in 1943.

The U.S. War Department agreed to take 1,500 AJAs (Americans of Japanese ancestry) into the U.S. Army. Some 10,000 AJAs in Hawaii volunteered; nearly 3,000 were accepted. That was the birth of Hawaii's 442nd Regimental Combat Team. In all, 33,000 nisei in the United States served in the military, including the men from Hawaii's battle-seasoned 100th Infantry, called "The Purple Heart Battalion," volunteers from relocation camps, and those who fought in the Military Intelligence

Hawaii's AJA volunteers assembled at the foot of Iolani Palace for a massive send-off on March 28, 1943. An editorial in the *Honolulu Star-Bulletin* said, "no scene in Honolulu during World War II has been more striking, more significant. . . ." The majority of the men formed the core of the 442nd Regimental Combat Team, while some served with intelligence and secret service units in the Pacific. *Hawaii State Archives Photo.*

Service (MIS) in the Pacific War. The work of the intelligence group, referred to as one of the best kept secrets of the war, is credited with saving thousands of lives and shortening the war.

Stanley joined the intelligence service. With him and twenty-one other Pahoa nisei in uniform, the war suddenly seemed even closer. Mr. James Lee, our social studies teacher, helped us to understand the war. He made phrases like "blitzkrieg" and "pincer movement" and alien places like Salerno and Guadalcanal come to life. I remember our joy when American troops defeated the Japanese at Midway in the turning-point battle of the Pacific War. I also recall our relief when Rommel was finally in retreat in North Africa.

The struggle that wasn't finished was the one over the way I felt about being Japanese. The U.S. government's actions against the Japanese Americans and things Japanese made it painfully "official" to me that being Japanese was anti-American. I stopped eating rice because it was the Japanese staple. I insisted that we have more American-type meals. I started cooking "American" dishes such as boiled tongue and sauteed beef liver, which I had just learned to make in Faye Oishi's home economics class. My brothers balked and I was forced to retreat to hamburgers and stews. The government posters said, "Speak American. Don't Speak the Enemy's Language." So I frustrated my mother terribly by speaking English to her, disregarding the fact that she, like the other issei, communicated primarily in Japanese.

Increasingly, I wanted to leave my village. It had been my whole world, but now I ached to go beyond Pahoa's tangerine trees. When I was in the eighth grade, I asked my mother if I could go to high school in Honolulu so that I could prepare for college to become a newspaper reporter—a choice inspired by the World War II writings of newspaperman Ernie Pyle and the fabled adventures of reporter Lois Lane of Superman comics. Then when I met my sister Ellen's teacher, Mrs. Yukino N. Fukabori, who wrote for the *Hilo Tribune Herald,* I knew that it was possible, especially because my family was so supportive.

I was to join Ellen and live with our eldest sister, Matsuko, and her husband, Shuji, in their home in McCully. I started getting ready to leave a year in advance. I was so preoccupied now I didn't think much about the war anymore, except when my brother Stanley's letters came from Camp Savage and Ft. Snelling in Minnesota or when Walter Shiigi was wounded in his leg while fighting in Italy. I wrote him a cheer-up letter. The war was going well for the allies and people were saying it was just a matter of time before total victory.

When the day finally came for me to say goodbye to my village and lifelong friends, I was surprised the leave-taking was not traumatic. I sailed aboard the old interisland steamer *Hualalai*. Too excited to sleep, I spent the night on deck, and in the quiet darkness I thought about my friends, my mother, and brothers Carl and Chip, two years older than I. I felt sad that I would not be helping my mother. I thought about Carl—he had been 9 or 10 that day I had walked into the house and found him standing so erect, his head tilted up, smiling proudly at an imaginary flag. His right hand was over his heart. He was so immersed in the "Star-Spangled Banner" playing on our old Zenith radio that he did not notice I had slipped in and out again, too embarrassed to show him how touched I was. How strange it would be not to see him—them—the next morning as I had all of my life. What would it be like to wake up in a world other than Pahoa?

With the first faint light of the new day, a floating Honolulu appeared, bathed in a glow of hazy pinks and lavenders. I felt that I was entering an enchanted land. (I was reminded of this scene in 1966 when one of the *Our House Divided* nisei I interviewed described the tender-awkward feelings that the first view of Honolulu evoked in him the morning he returned from war.)

When the *Hualalai* docked at Honolulu Harbor in the mugginess of late August, I thought how different it must have been when my father's ship entered the same harbor in 1898, and my mother's in 1913.

My sisters Ellen (nicknamed "H" for Hanako) and Matsuko

("M") spotted me first. They waved and could not hold back their giggles as I walked down the gangplank wearing a pair of red slacks, saddle oxfords, and a woolen pullover the color of strawberry sherbet under a heavy coral pink woolen coat lined in rose satin. I had loved that coat the first time I saw it in a shop window in Hilo and had talked my mother into buying it for me. I think she understood that the coat, despite the sweltering August weather, was important to me as a symbol of my growing up, leaving home, and going far away. I was crossing the ocean, after all.

Honolulu was like stepping into a Ginger Rogers movie: women in clicking high heels and snug-fitting dresses, men in wingtip shoes and blockbuster ties, all against a backdrop of buildings taller than Pahoa's Catholic Church steeple lined with spotless show windows that fronted streets bustling with so many cars, growling buses, and sleek taxis. I awoke each day at a half-run to explore the huge libraries, markets with bin upon bin of fresh produce, Japanese delicatessens called *okazuya* that sold sushi and shrimp tempura every day of the week, the incredible beauty of the turquoise sea rolling onto white sand beaches—not black sand as in Kalapana and Kapoho on the Big Island, and downtown streets jammed with servicemen talking boisterously above the din of jukeboxes in the bars and snack shops.

I realized much later what I wasn't aware of then, that sometime during the transition—from my village to the city—I had buried the jumble of pain I had harbored since the war started. I apparently had turned my attention to becoming as "American" as I could.

Ironically, McKinley High School, where I spent the next three years, was nicknamed "Tokyo High" because of the high proportion of Japanese American students. It was not until I began doing research for this book that I realized what a critical part McKinley and its beloved principal Miles E. Cary played in bringing public educational opportunities to the children of immigrants, over the strenuous opposition of Hawaii's oligarchy. According to Fuchs, in *Hawaii Pono,* the powers-that-be felt that education would "destroy an economy based on the utilization of masses of ignorant laborers."

Fuchs found that public education in Hawaii prospered because of Cary's leadership and the excellence of the teachers of the 1920s and 1930s. He said: "Probably no community in the world was blessed with so devoted a group of educators as were the Islands during those two decades."

To me, in the fall of 1944, McKinley was simply a big new experience. It was well over ten times larger than Pahoa School, and the size of the student body was perhaps three times Pahoa's entire population of under a thousand.

I fell easily into McKinley's rhythm: writing essays like "What the United States Navy Means to Me"; wearing rolled-up jeans and baggy shirts to the Black and Gold's football games, which I attended with my best chum Rose Lee; working in the pineapple fields once a week for the "war effort"; wishing that cute fellow in Latin would notice me.

On April 12, 1945, President Franklin Delano Roosevelt died and the entire student body sadly sang his favorite song, "Home on the Range." Less than a month later on May 7 came V-E Day, Germany's surrender. Hawaii went right on working and began gearing up for an expected all-out effort in the Pacific War with Hawaii as a vital base. War workers in Hawaii criticized the mainland for celebrating prematurely because clearly the war was not over for Hawaii.

But V-J Day—the day that Japan surrendered—three months later was quite another story. Then Hawaii joined the rest of the United States and the allied world and celebrated jubilantly. The end of the war in Japan, of course, was far from jubilant. Some of the family members I interviewed for *Our House Divided* described the great despair—and relief.

I was in Pahoa that summer. There was no big merrymaking in our village. The old metal alarm that had clanged the start of the war now clanged to mark its end. As I look back I realize how layered with emotions V-J Day was in Pahoa. People were relieved—the boys would be coming home, and so would those who were interned. But there was sadness, too. Kazumi Tsutsui of Pahoa and Tadao Nakamura of neighboring Kapoho had been killed in battle. And there was anxiety. Our family and the issei community were worried about the mysterious atomic bomb that American planes had dropped on Hiroshima on August 6, 1945, and on Nagasaki on August 8, that led to Japan's surrender. What had happened to my father and grandparents? The anxiety was not ours alone. Hiroshima Prefecture had been the biggest single source of Japanese immigrants in Hawaii. The Red Cross network was swamped with queries. Another worry was that we had not heard from Stanley for many weeks. Had he been shipped out to Japan and, if so, was he safe? News reports said the new bomb had the power of 20,000 tons of TNT. I had no idea what one stick of dynamite could do, let alone 20,000 tons.

(But after interviewing Robert Fujiwara and others for *Our House Divided,* I not only got an idea of the destructive force of an atom bomb, but also came to understand what the bomb does to human life and human spirit.)

In Pahoa that night I celebrated V-J Day by going to sleep singing to myself, "When the lights go on again all over the world . . ." Through the open window I could smell the country air and watch the wind making dancers of the gauzy, white curtains again. In that brief moment everything seemed as it had been before—when I was 11 and everything was forever. Now I was almost 16.

The formal Japanese surrender came on September 1, 1945, aboard the battleship *Missouri* in Tokyo Bay. Author Gwenfread Allen writes in *Hawaii's War Years 1941–1945* that the event was celebrated in Honolulu with a giant victory parade featuring 30,000 representatives from all of Hawaii's ethnic groups, "except the Japanese."

We then received a wire from the International Red Cross that my father had died of natural causes in Hiroshima on February 3, 1943, nine days before his sixty-seventh birthday. I felt sad. I always knew my father's health would not improve, only worsen, and I had wished privately that he could die before conditions in wartime Japan deteriorated to the point where nourishing food and medical care would not be available. I was glad he had been spared from the Hiroshima bombing.

Our spirits lifted when we received word from Stanley. He was with the U.S. Occupation forces in Japan. He wrote that our relatives lived on the outskirts of Hiroshima and had escaped the bombing. He said that when he went there my fisherman grandfather, still jaunty at 73, had greeted him as he always had in Hawaii: "Oh, Yoshinori (Stanley's Japanese name), you've come home."

Stanley described his confusing emotions upon visiting our father's grave; his visit ended with a feeling of forgiving peace. I, too, was to experience a mixture of emotions twenty-one years later on my first trip to Japan, when I stood in silent Buddhist prayer at his gravesite in a serene valley fringed by shade trees. I was full of regret that my father and I had had so little time together and that I had not been able to help him in his last days.

The end of the war, the end of worrying about my father and grandparents, was a relief, like a drenching rain after a siege of sticky weather.

Shortly after Japan's surrender, bizarre rumors started to circulate among the issei—that Japan, not America, had won the war, and that the victorious Japanese fleet would be arriving at Pearl Harbor soon to take over the Islands. I heard a neighbor intently giving some of this misinformation to my mother. I reacted by laughing. Then I felt irritated at such embarrassing nonsense. My mother assured me she was not taken in by the rumor, but cautioned me not to make fun of those who did because they were old and needed time to get over the shock.

The episode provided insight into how difficult the war must have been for the issei, who were caught in the middle of a bitter battle between the two nations they were so strongly attached to: one, their motherland, where close family members still lived, and the other, the land where they had spent most of

A scene from the Japanese-language version of Teruaki Miyata's *The
Defeated,* a play about the demoralizing aftermath of Japan's World War
II defeat, which was staged in Japanese at the University of Hawaii in
1948 under the auspices of the nisei veterans of Club 100. Here Albert
Miyasato, whose story is told in Chapter 5, plays the lead role, a Japanese
soldier who returns home and despairs at the terrible consequences of the
war and defeat he sees around him. June Arakaki (now Arakawa) plays
the young woman who gives him hope. At *left* is her younger sister, played
by Yasuko Saito. Japanese and English versions of the play, both directed
by Professor Earle Ernst, who was in charge of theatrical censorship with
the U.S. Occupation forces, were performed at the university. The play
was originally entitled *Omoide* (Remembrances). *Miyasato Photo Collection.*

their lives and had raised their children in communities they had
helped to build and shape. When the false rumors first emerged,
issei like my mother were able to sort out fact from fiction. Others who got drawn into the delusion were snapped out of it by
their nisei children, who would not tolerate such foolishness. A
small core of fanatics, however, persisted for years. One group
called itself the Hawaii Hisshokai (Hawaii Victory Society).

As I did my research for this book, I understood better how

very painful it must have been for the older Japanese to accept a defeated Japan. When they came to Hawaii and were treated badly, Japan had been a constant source of support. It gave the immigrants a needed sense of protection and identity, a bond that the Japanese government fostered among her overseas "children." When harsh Hawaii and U.S. laws continued to be imposed to hold the Japanese down, including the denial of citizenship, resentment fueled pro-Japan patriotism in some Hawaii Japanese circles.

As Professor John J. Stephan of the University of Hawaii states in his book, *Hawaii under the Rising Sun—Japan's Plans for Conquest after Pearl Harbor,* Japanese American loyalty was not a black and white issue. The situation in Hawaii, he says, was "very complex. . . . An intricate web of human ties bound Hawaii to both sides of the Pacific."

There were a few Hawaii Japanese who had cast their loyalty with Japan by choice. Others, caught in Japan when the war started, fought and worked for Japan not exactly by choice. A few in internment and evacuation camps elected to expatriate or repatriate, often out of anger or despair. There were issei who were sympathetic to Japan, and there were nisei who fought for the right to volunteer for combat to prove their loyalty to America.

That complexity is what this book is about.

My personal recollection of what went on in our community is that people like my mother, who had their hands too full just coping with day-to-day living, didn't have time to indulge in patriotic politics. To the working class mainstream in which I grew up, the issei's most important loyalty was not to a country, but to their children—to bring them up with good values, to educate them, and to help them succeed in the American system. For my mother, personal ties to Japan were important, but Japan was a part of her past. American Hawaii was the present and future for her, just as it was for her children.

In 1980 Congress established the U.S. Commission on Wartime Relocation and Internment of Civilians. The report that the commission published in 1982 stated that not a single act of espionage, sabotage, or fifth column activity had been committed by Americans of Japanese ancestry or by resident Japanese aliens on the West Coast or in Hawaii.

After lengthy investigation the commission found that the acts of exclusion, removal, and detention of Japanese Americans during the war were not justified by military necessity. It found that "a grave injustice" had been done to the Japanese Americans; the reasons behind those acts were "race prejudice, war hysteria, and a failure of political leadership." Among recommendations the commission made as "an act of national apology," was compensatory payment of $20,000 to each of about sixty thousand survivors. The first of these payments was made in October 1990 to the oldest survivors. Among them was Mrs. Haru Tanaka, then 97, whose story is a part of this book.

The nation's formal apology to the Japanese Americans, in a congressional bill signed by President Reagan in 1988, finally lifted the stigma of disloyalty and enabled the Japanese to begin healing their psychic wounds. The healing process actually had begun long before when the AJAs won the nation's respect through their stunning combat achievements in the Pacific and Europe. The showpiece was the 442nd Regimental Combat Team, celebrated as the most decorated unit of World War II. Its honors included seven Presidential Unit Citations, the last of which was presented by President Harry S. Truman on July 15, 1946, at a special review on the White House lawn. In making the presentation, the president said: "You fought for the free nations of the world. . . . You fought not only the enemy, you fought prejudice, and you have won. Keep up that fight, and continue to win—to make this great Republic stand for just what the Constitution says it stands for: 'the welfare of all of the people, all of the time.' "

Four of the seven *Our House Divided* families had sons who served in the American military, including three with the 442nd and two with intelligence units in the Pacific. Katsugo Miho, who served with the 442nd, describes the restless tension after the war as he and the other vets worked through their "re-entry blues" and Hawaii's adjustment to peacetime. Even in Pahoa I could sense the shifting mood during my last summer there in 1946, before my mother and two brothers moved to Honolulu. Gone was the boisterous excitement of the mainland GIs, who left as they had come—in truckloads. Now there was the edginess of the returning veterans, who no longer fitted into the plantation scheme of things. Also, sugar plantation labor unions, repressed during the war, revved up for strike action, which came that fall and culminated with an impressive victory that ended plantation paternalism in Hawaii.

For me that summer was tinged with sadness. I knew that this village would never be my home again.

Pahoa receded in my memory once I began to study at the University of Hawaii, which was dominated in the late 1940s by war veterans taking advantage of educational benefits under the GI Bill. A standout even then was Dan Inouye, now U.S. Senator Inouye, who wore a black-gloved prosthesis in place of the right arm he had lost in combat with the 442nd two weeks before the war ended. He always appeared, well, senatorial, with an entourage of veterans around him.

My newspaper career started as a reporter for the university's student newspaper, *Ka Leo,* and as a university columnist and summer reporter for the *Honolulu Advertiser.* My paycheck as a reporter was $52 a month. That was heady stuff for the girl from Pahoa.

My twenty-five-year love affair with the *Honolulu Star-Bulletin* began on May 5, 1952, in a crowded and steamy City Room, noisy with the clatter of linotype machines, at 125 Merchant Street in the heart of the downtown financial district. That day was one of the happiest days in my life. I wanted to be the best reporter I could be. And I was lucky because the editors of my formative newspaper years were not only superb at their craft, but also held to high ethical standards that guarded against editorial compromise.

Even as I absorbed this City Room idealism, I was aware of

the less-than-ideal realities in the world outside, such as America's "Red hunts" of the 1950s, the consequences of America's A-bomb devastation, and the problem of resettlement for the thousands of Japanese Americans who still struggled with racial hostility in California. There was racial prejudice in Hawaii, too. Among the more publicized cases during this period was the Outrigger Canoe Club's refusal to admit internationally acclaimed swimmer Keo Nakama as a luncheon guest because he was Japanese. Another case was author James Michener's report of racial discrimination in Hawaii against him and his Japanese American wife, Mari. Michener said that property in certain districts was off-limits to people of Asian ancestry, as were the best clubs in Honolulu. During that time a friend of mine was warned by the Waikiki Yacht Club that if he continued to take his ethnic mix of friends out on his sailboat against the club's whites-only policy, he would be blackballed.

But even as the racist dramas played themselves out, a bigger drama began unfolding in the Hawaii of the 1950s—one that the "five percent" haole elite had feared and had tried strenuously to block: the rise of the Japanese American in business, the professions, and especially in politics.

The young AJA lions, now equipped with their degrees, were ready to make good their foxhole promises to bring about social reforms and to open the door of equal opportunity so long denied them and their parents. Hawaii's Democratic Party became their political vehicle. They rallied under the leadership of John A. Burns, an ex-policeman who had been among the defenders of Hawaii's Japanese during the war. They formed a coalition with organized labor and committed individuals to build up the barely breathing Democratic Party.

First the AJAs worked to get Congress to grant the issei the right to U.S. citizenship. This was achieved at long last in 1952. Being barred from citizenship was the most significant wrong done to the issei. It kept them out of the political process and left them defenseless against discrimination.

The opening wedge in Hawaii politics came in 1954 when

the new Democratic leadership toppled the reign of the Republicans in Hawaii by winning control of the Territorial Legislature. Nearly half of the seats were won by nisei. The Democratic tide swept Burns in as Hawaii's delegate to Congress in 1956. He brought home the long-awaited prize of statehood for Hawaii in 1959—which finally assured political equality for all —particularly to the Asians, who had been treated as second-class citizens for so long.

It was in the midst of this harvest season for the Japanese Americans in Hawaii in the fall of 1966 that I found a note stuck in my typewriter from my then managing editor, A. A. (Bud) Smyser, asking that we meet with Editor William H. Ewing to discuss an upcoming assignment. The assignment was to locate Japanese families that had been divided between the United States and Japan as a result of World War II and then to write a series of stories to mark the twenty-fifth anniversary of Pearl Harbor.

My search for divided families started in our newspaper files. I could not find a single clipping on the subject. Neither could I locate any reference to such families in our historical resources. Calls to the Japanese Chamber of Commerce, the U.S. Immigration and Naturalization Service, and the Japanese Consulate produced no results. Bud came up with a possibility: Attorney Katsuro Miho's family. It checked out. That was the groundbreaker. After that, one lead led to another and then another. Soon I had the names of ten families. After eliminating those without addresses and known relatives, I ended up with seven families.

I began my interviews in Hawaii and made arrangements for corresponding interviews in Japan and on the mainland. The two serious problems I anticipated in Japan—language and logistics—were resolved when my brother Stanley agreed to assist me. He had remained in Japan with a U.S. Air Force intelligence agency after finishing his tour of duty with the Occupation forces. He scheduled my interviews across Japan. As an interpreter Stanley was superb, alert to the nuances and idiosyncrasies of speech on both sides.

For most of the people whom I interviewed in the United States and Japan, this was the first telling of what had been a fearful and trying chapter in their lives. Again and again they referred to their self-imposed silence. They said they had felt it was best to forget and to go on with their lives. Thoughts and emotions sealed within them for twenty-five years poured out fresh without the patina of practiced retellings. I felt privileged to witness their reactions firsthand.

The interviews inspired me in a way that was not immediately clear. From each person came courage, humility, and discipline. Imagine the former Islander who had stared into the past as he told of the paralyzing moment when he, a soldier in the Imperial Japanese Army, had spotted his older brother from Hawaii in the uniform of the U.S. Army. Imagine the Wahiawa mother who recalled that day in a bleak Texas internment camp surrounded by barbed wire. Her worries about her daughter stranded in Japan were interrupted by a letter from her only son. It began: "I am now an American soldier. I must fight and, if necessary, die for my country." Imagine the toughest of the interviews—the young man who had grown up on the island of Hawaii and was drafted into the Japanese army. He lay near death for months after being pulled out of one of the worst areas of the Hiroshima atomic bombing. Twenty-one years had not dimmed his pain or anxiety.

It was only after I had interviewed him and had gone through the Hiroshima Peace Museum that I finally grasped what had happened there that day in August 1945. I felt such a sadness I could not speak for hours; all I could do was weep. The same sadness has returned each of the four times I went back to the museum. And each time, I felt that the cause of peace would be well served if it were compulsory for all leaders of the world to visit the museum.

Except for the young man who was so gravely injured in the atomic holocaust, the timing was right for the interviews. Sufficient time had passed to enable those I interviewed to have gained a degree of distance without the blurring of memory. I am convinced that in addition to the natural healing that came with time, the enormous leap in the status of the Japanese in Hawaii was a big factor in enabling them to feel secure enough to probe their deep wounds.

The intensity of their experiences or the intensity unleashed in their telling gave to me a special clarity. When I returned from Japan and started composing, their stories seemed almost to write themselves.

The series began in the *Honolulu Star-Bulletin* as scheduled on December 7, 1966. We were gratified at readers' responses through their letters and telephone calls. At the urging of several Hawaii and mainland writers, my editors attempted to have the stories published as a book, but publishers in New York then rejected the idea on grounds the subject was "too sensitive." I promised myself that I would get the book published someday. That day is here.

# Chapter 1

## THE MIHO STORY

It was a warm mid-autumn day in Tokyo in 1966. Fumiye Miho, a member of Hawaii's Miho family, tugged her sweater close to her as she remembered a similar September day in Tokyo in 1945.

She said that for the first time in what seemed like years, though it was only days, she had let herself forget about A-bombs, death, and destruction, the evidence of defeat all around her. "I just wanted to enjoy the sunshine and forget the war for a moment," she said, "when suddenly, I froze. I was covered with goose bumps and I trembled with fear. I had just had my first look at American GIs and I was terrified."

"Imagine!" she said, "Me! Born and raised in Hawaii! Afraid at the sight of Americans! That remembrance still makes me shiver. It seemed that all my schizophrenic feelings about the United States and Japan confronted me in that chilling moment in 1945. I had actually come to believe all the Japanese propaganda without realizing it," she said. "The propagandists had pounded over and over again that if American troops got into Japan, the GIs would rape all the women. Women were advised to look as dirty as possible.

"Even in the dying days of the war, the propagandists kept saying that Japan was winning. Imagine them saying that in the face of all the evidence showing otherwise. And yet, I believed the propaganda," she said.

"Many times, I've tried to analyze why my feelings toward the United States and Japan were what they were. I think part of it was that, all the while I grew up, I saw racial inequality around me. The haoles up there and the Orientals down here. I saw all the injustice. I wanted to go to Japan. In my heart, I felt that as a Japanese in Japan, I wouldn't be treated as a second-class citizen."

And so, shortly after graduating from the University of Hawaii in 1939, she went to Japan to teach English at a women's college, on the invitation of a visiting philosopher. Ironically, it was the same perception of racial inequality and the need to prove their loyalty to the United States that spurred three of her brothers—Katsuro, Katsuaki, and Katsugo—along with 10,000 other Island nisei, to volunteer to fight for America. Of that number almost 3,000 were selected and formed the nucleus of what history now refers to as "the famed 442nd Regimental Combat Team."

Katsuro, an attorney, was rejected by the army, but served the community in various ways, like working with the wartime Emergency Service Committee, the Hawaii Statehood Commission, and the City Planning Commission. He also worked with community leaders to lay the early groundwork for legislation that finally allowed Orientals to become U.S. citizens as of 1952.

Katsuaki and Katsugo were accepted for service. It was in a traffic accident during training that Katsuaki was killed at 24. The brothers had volunteered despite the fact that their father, Katsuichi Miho, had been taken at bayonet point on December 7, 1941, from his home in Kahului, Maui. He was detained in an alien internment camp on the mainland for the duration of the war.

The elder Miho, a former Japanese school teacher, had operated a store and a hotel. He had served as a volunteer for the Japanese Consulate and had been outspoken in his pro-Japan views.

Katsuro, the oldest son, said in an interview in Honolulu, "My father left home that day, thinking that he was going to be killed. To his family, he said: 'Don't do anything that will bring

Katsuro Miho, c. 1962.
*Star-Bulletin Photo.*

shame to the family and the Japanese race. Do your best no matter what. Keep your self-dignity.' " Katsuro said, "My father repeated what he had always told us: 'My country is Japan, but your country is the United States. No matter what happens to me, your country is the United States.' "

Katsuro noted that in those days, it was impossible under law for Japanese aliens to become naturalized citizens. He said that when the three brothers had volunteered for service, some federal officials talked about releasing Mr. Miho in the custody of his sons. "But," Katsuro recalled, "my father wouldn't leave unless the twenty or so others interned from Maui could leave, too. All or nothing."

Much to the elder Miho's surprise, he not only survived the internment experience, but enjoyed several aspects of it. He liked to jokingly refer to it as "a vacation at government expense." He often told his sons about the beautiful mountains of Missoula, Montana, and making illegal rice wine while the guards watched. He even sent samples of dried trout that he had caught. When he returned to Honolulu, he worked at a maca-

Katsuichi Miho on a snowy day at the Missoula, Montana, internment camp, 1944 or 1945. *Miho Photo Collection.*

damia nut farm on Round Top Drive and much later founded the Kaimuki Japanese Language School. He died in 1966 at age 82.

"He was quite a guy," said Katsugo, the youngest son and a state legislator for five terms. Katsugo said in an interview in Honolulu, "My father and mother's ethic about doing our duty for our country left no question about what we should do when the time came to act." Not surprisingly, all the Miho men have names beginning with the Japanese character *katsu,* which means loyalty.

On December 7, 1941, Katsugo was living at Atherton House (dormitory) at the University of Hawaii. He said, "I was shaving when one of the fellows yelled: 'It's war! The Japanese are attacking Pearl Harbor!' I didn't finish shaving and ran with the rest up on the roof to see black smoke rising out of Pearl Harbor. I wasn't shocked when war came, but I was shocked at the manner in which it came.

"I had felt that war was inevitable," he said. "The way relations between the two countries were going, something was bound to happen. I had tried not to think what that something would be. But attacking Pearl Harbor? I never imagined such a thing.

"My anxiety and frustration were relieved when the radio called all university ROTC students to assemble in the gym. Right away, we got guard duty under the just-born Hawaii Territorial Guard. We got rifles, although many of us didn't know how to fire them, and five rounds of ammunition."

While Katsugo did guard duty, Katsuaki, who was later accepted for medical school, worked long hours with the emergency medical crews. Then, about three months later, Katsugo and the other guardsmen were told to pack up and assemble. Katsugo said, "I'll never forget that man's honesty. Major Frazier. He came right out and laid the cards on the table. He told us we had to leave the guard because we were Japanese. He told us it was distasteful to him and that the local officers had protested the order, but that somebody up there wouldn't budge."

After that his nisei friends formed the Varsity Victory Volunteers work battalion. Katsugo left for Maui to help his mother run the family hotel. He and his brothers were amazed at just how much their mother could endure without bitterness, without complaints. Katsugo did defense work on Maui, building facilities at the Puunene Naval Air Station and the Kahului

Naval Air Station. He joined the 442nd the moment the U.S. Army opened its doors to nisei in March of 1943.

Fumiye Miho said the war shouldn't have come as a surprise to her either, because she had lived through all the warning signs in Tokyo: the gradual military takeover; the Gestapo-like fears that the "walls have ears"; the movement early in 1941 to stop people from speaking or looking like Americans; the frightening moment on the train when an elderly man yelled "*bakayaro* [you fool]" because she had on a stylish, frilly American hat then in vogue; the urging by the American Consulate for all Americans to return to the United States.

"But," Fumiye said, "I just wouldn't let myself believe it could really happen."

When the attack on Pearl Harbor occurred, she was teaching English to a group of White Russian refugee children in a Greek Orthodox church in Tokyo. She said a Miss Zabriaski came running across the room and said, "Miss Miho, Miss Miho, war between Japan and the United States."

"I assured her, 'It's just propaganda. Don't believe it', and went right on teaching. But when I left the church, the blare of military music filled the streets. I rushed home and flung the door open. My sister, Tsukie, and I ran into each other's arms and cried. What we had feared in our hearts had come true."

For Fumiye, a dual citizen, the war years were a jarring blur of dissonance, disorder, and despair. She lost her teaching job because English was now forbidden. She was assigned to work in the information office of the Japanese cabinet. But the unending bombings later caused her to evacuate to the outskirts of Hiroshima to her sister Hisae's home.

She said, "By July of 1945, it was clear that the end was near for Japan. But the news on the radio and in the newspapers kept saying that Japan was winning—and I believed them. I was a perfect victim of propaganda. The rumor was that Japan wanted to decoy American troops into the Japanese mainland. The people armed themselves with bamboo poles in preparation for the American coming. There were those who felt that

Japan was losing. To them, I would say, 'You're only drinking in American propaganda'—little realizing that I was drunk with Japanese propaganda. In fact, some Japanese would say to me: 'My, Miho-*sensei* [teacher], you talk like you're a native Japanese and we talk like we're Americans.' "

While their sister was shifting her loyalty more and more to Japan, Katsugo and Katsuaki fought desperately to prove their American loyalty. They trained at Camp Shelby in Mississippi. Their first battle was to win the confidence and respect of white fellow soldiers and the people of Mississippi.

Katsugo recalled, "We used to have knock-down, drag-out fights every time someone called us 'Japs'. We just couldn't take that. We had to prove ourselves not only in battle, but in our own camp."

The brothers went to see their father in an internment camp in Alexandria, Louisiana. Katsugo said, "They called it an internment camp, but for all intents and purposes, it was a POW camp with guard towers and barbed wire. Guards stood by as relatives visited at a long table split by a wooden partition. Visitors and inmates spoke to each other over this partition." He said, "Tragically funny were the signs all around that said 'Speak English Only'. The inmates, of course, were aliens who spoke little if any English.

"When the officer of the day saw that we were American soldiers, he let us have complete freedom of the room. My father told us the U.S. Army treated them well. He wanted to know how we liked army life. He reminded us about doing our duty well and not disgracing the family." Katsugo said: "My father didn't talk about it, but I knew that he was not just worried about us, but also about his children in Japan."

In addition to Fumiye, the Mihos had two other daughters, Hisae and Rosaline Tsukie, in Japan. Tsukie went to Japan after high school in Hawaii and married a dentist in Tokyo. Because she was born in Japan, she was unable to become a U.S. citizen. Hisae and another son, Katsuto, were born in Japan and had never been to Hawaii. Katsuto died in 1927.

Brothers Katsugo, *left,* and Katsuaki Miho in June 1943 while in training at Camp Shelby, Mississippi. Katsuaki died in a highway accident several months later. *Miho Photo Collection.*

Hisae married a school teacher who served in the Japanese army and died as a Russian POW during the war.

Katsugo saw his father again in the fall of 1943. This time it was at a camp in Missoula, Montana. It was a sad mission. He took the ashes of his brother, Katsuaki, who had died in a highway truck accident while on temporary duty in Dolton, Alabama. Memorial services were held in the Ft. Missoula internment camp. Katsugo remembers how astonished the guards were. "They asked me why had we volunteered to fight for the American Army while the American Army held our father in captivity. They just couldn't figure that out." The urn of ashes was taken to the Mihos' other son, Paul Katsuso, a minister with the University of Hawaii's YMCA, who was then studying at the Yale Divinity School. Paul brought the ashes back to Hawaii later for burial in the Punchbowl Memorial Cemetery of the Pacific.

Katsugo remembered how "terribly downhearted my father was over the death. I think he would have accepted my brother's death better if he had died in battle. My father felt that for my brother to die in a highway accident was a double waste of a son who had held so much promise."

Katsugo said that just about that time Katsuro wrote saying how upset he was because federal officials suspected that their

Mr. and Mrs. Katsuichi Miho visiting their son Katsuaki's grave at the Punchbowl Memorial Cemetery in Honolulu after the war. *Miho Photo Collection.*

sister, Fumiye, was Tokyo Rose. Various people who had known her in Hawaii listened to Rose's recorded voice and testified that the voice didn't belong to Fumiye. Katsugo said, "It seems funny now, but it wasn't then."

In April of 1944, the 442nd crossed the Atlantic in a large convoy. The team moved through strange towns with unfamiliar names—Palermo, Brindisi, Civitavecchia, Naples, Anzio, Strasbourg, Mannheim, Stuttgart, Munich, Berchtesgaden, Nice, Monte Carlo, and on and on. Its baptismal fire came in Belvedere near Rome. Then came the bloody battles of Hill 140, Cecina, Leghorn, Pisa, and Florence in Italy. The team went on to France, where the 442nd had its costliest battle in the rescue of the "Texas Lost Battalion" in the Vosges Mountains. The "Champagne Campaign" in the French Riviera gave the AJAs the chance to get rest-and-recreation passes to Nice, where they remembered momentarily how to forget.

In March of 1945, Katsugo's artillery unit took part in the invasion of Germany which ended with V-E Day on May 7. He recalls the end of that war as "sober and sobering." Along the roadside on the outskirts of Munich and in the paradoxically heavenly countryside of Berchtesgaden were the Jews, "roaming like lost sheep—the living dead. They had been liberated from what we understood was the nearby Nazi concentration camp of Dachau."

Katsugo said that two members of their advance party, including Shozo Kajioka of Hawaii, shot open the locks to the concentration camp gate and out poured the Jews. "Hundreds of them," Katsugo said. "It was a sight that burned in our minds. Skin and bones that once were men. I wondered if they could ever recover. We spent the days giving them C rations. All our rations. There was a little snow still on the ground. And we saw some of them going after carcasses of horses and cows in the field."

Katsugo stayed with the occupation forces in Germany until December 1945. Finally, it was time to head home. Katsugo said, "It seemed unreal—so unreal that most of us got on the troopship SS *Erickson* in Marseilles bound for New York as if we were heading for another campaign. But once on the ship, we knew this one was different. There was a lot of singing— mostly off-key. Glenn Miller tunes like 'Slow Boat to China'." He said, "I think we all had a lump in our throat when we got our first sight of a foggy New York."

They flew to California and boarded the troopship SS *New Mexico* for the final lap of the voyage home to Pier 40 in Honolulu Harbor. Among the four hundred or so returning AJAs were nisei like Ted Tsukiyama, who was recruited out of Camp Shelby for the Military Intelligence Service in the Pacific. People didn't know about their work because the men were told not to talk about it. They were America's "secret weapon against the Japanese," Katsugo said.

At 3 A.M. January 14, 1946, the first lights of Honolulu were visible. Katsugo and the rest got out of their bunks. Their eyes stayed glued on the city. They kidded each other, trying to conceal their nervousness and to hold back the flood of feelings that were ready to burst through. The ship pulled into the harbor. They were really home.

The dockside was packed with people. The Royal Hawaiian Band was in full swing. The perfume and vibrant colors of leis were everywhere. And vats of joyful tears. In the middle of all this, Katsugo said, "came the shock of realizing that I had not really expected to come back again—ever."

Then came the slow adjustment. The difficult re-entry. "Like learning to walk again." Katsugo recalled how a group of them would meet in town every day at the pool hall of the Owl Cafe on Bethel Street. On Saturdays they held a beer bust at Sandy Beach. Very gradually, the group thinned out as some of them got jobs, others found girlfriends or got married, and the rest went back to the University of Hawaii.

Katsugo remembers how hard it was to study. "Just couldn't study. Couldn't settle down. It took a good year." After the University of Hawaii, he went to George Washington University Law School under the GI Bill.

In Japan, the end of the war was vastly different. There were no leis and no band music, but lots of tears, rubble, and despair.

Fumiye said, "It was sheer accident that I had missed the train that would have taken me from my tiny village to Hiroshima City that August morning in 1945. From the train station miles away from the city, I heard the noise. I saw the blinding flash and the tulip shape of pastel-colored smoke floating into the sky. I thought to myself: 'My, those Americans are using beautiful camouflage.' "

In the afternoon, rumors poured into the village that Hiroshima had been wiped out and that practically everyone had died from a strange bomb.

"I saw trucks loaded with victims that evening. The only medication we had were bottles of mercurochrome. Families couldn't recognize their own relatives. A horrendous mess of burned bodies.

"It doesn't make any sense when you think of it now," she said, "but the next day, I felt I must go to work in the city. The train stopped mid-way and I walked many miles the rest of the way. I couldn't believe the destruction. In the bombings of Tokyo, there was always that vivacity of life as the living hustled to put out fires, dig for belongings, and rush to escape. But in Hiroshima, it was different. Everyone was just lying down. The whole atmosphere spoke of death. The unlivingness of it all.

"It was destruction with a capital D. Annihilation. Corpses lay around. No one knew what to do. It was so inconceivable. I stayed there to help feed victims canned juice through paper funnels. For several nights, I slept on the grass. Soon, the stench of the dead was overwhelming. They burned the bodies. Piles of unclaimed bodies.

"When I returned home, my grandmother turned white and said, 'Obake daro? [Are you a ghost?].' She thought I had died in the blast."

Fumiye said that shortly afterward "we were told to straighten our collar and give our utmost attention to a radio broadcast that day. We were stunned when the emperor spoke to announce the surrender. His voice sounded wobbly and I could make out only one word, '*chin*', which is the emperor's term for 'I'."

So, it was all over except for the burden of defeat.

Fumiye worked as an interpreter for Japanese military officials during the demobilization. She and the rest of the Japanese who had expected the very worst marveled at the decency of the American Occupation. She said a Japanese general was again and again impressed at the respect Americans showed the defeated people. He noted how differently the conquering Japanese had treated the defeated Chinese in earlier times. She could remember only one humiliating instance when an American general refused to even look up when a Japanese general paid him a call. The American general also rejected a traditional Japanese gift presented to him at the time.

But that was an exception. Her memories were filled with warmer remembrances. She recalled the young American soldier who stopped her one day, in spite of the U.S. Army's firm antifraternization order. She said he was so insecure and so lonely. He just wanted someone to talk with.

"My friends and I decided to take him to a show," she said. "In the theatre, I felt a tap on my shoulder. Sitting behind me was an old Hawaii friend, Charles Murashige. From him, I learned of my father's internment, Katsuaki's death, Katsugo's service with the 442nd, and Paul's marriage to a caucasian woman. I felt a tremendous amount of guilt.

"In the silence of that sleepless night, I thought of many things. Slowly, gradually, I tore myself apart to find out who I was and what I stood for. After agonizingly painful self-examination, I felt I must regain my U.S. citizenship and find its true meaning." She returned to Hawaii, and in the years following she continued to probe deeply into the meaning of her existence. She studied Christianity at Yale Divinity School, and in 1950 she abandoned Buddhism, a faith she had long embraced, and chose to become a Quaker.

Fumiye Miho being inter-
viewed in Tokyo in 1966.
*Star-Bulletin Photo.*

She said, "I believe in the Quakers' emphasis on peace. To me, human commitment to peace is the true meaning of the Christian faith."

She then returned to Japan as a missionary and later headed the Friends Center in Tokyo. Her hope for peace is for people to come to an understanding through dialogue.

As the interview concluded, she thought again about that September morning of 1945 when she erupted in goose bumps at the sight of American GIs. "That was a long time ago," she said.

This time she didn't shiver at the memory.

# 1990 Update

Fumiye Miho, 76, is now in her fortieth year of work for peace in Japan. She has retired as the head of the Friends Center in Tokyo, but has continued to live and teach at the girls school there. She also carries on her peace work through the YWCA, the International Christian College, and Sophia University in Tokyo.

Mrs. Ayano Miho died in 1967 at the age of 80. Her daughter Hisae Miho Okada died in Hiroshima in 1980 at the age of 72. She is survived by four children.

Tsukie Miho Fujimori, 80, who formerly lived in Tokyo, now makes her home in Honolulu. So does her daughter.

Katsuro, 78, has retired from the practice of law and lives in Honolulu with his wife, Jayne. They have two sons.

Paul, 74, has retired as a curriculum specialist with the Hawaii Department of Education. He was for many years the executive secretary of the YMCA's Atherton House for University of Hawaii students. He and his wife, Ruth, have three sons and a daughter.

Katsugo, 68, is the executive assistant to the president of Servco Pacific, Inc. He served as a District Family Court judge from 1971 to 1979. He and his wife, Laura, have three daughters and a son. He is a Hawaii Housing Authority commissioner and is active in a number of community organizations.

# Chapter 2

■

# THE ASAMI STORY

It was midnight, December 7, 1941. Two FBI men rapped on the door of the newly built, white, frame cottage in Kaimuki, a suburb of Honolulu. A middle-aged man in pajamas answered the door.

"Are you Shoichi Asami?" one of the FBI men asked as he flashed his badge.

"Yes," Asami replied, and before he could ask what the meaning of all this was, the bigger of the FBI men ordered, "Get dressed. You have to come with us as an alien internee of war."

Asami, 47, managing editor of the Japanese section of the bilingual *Hawaii Times* newspaper, didn't need any further explanation. He realized this was war; he was an official of a Japanese language newspaper that held pro-Japan views. Asami asked, "What about my wife? My children?"

One of the FBI men shook his head: "No, just you. Get dressed right away."

Asami put his suit on. His wife, Shizu, 43, nervously helped him. He assured her, "Don't worry . . . everything will be all right . . . take care of the children." With that, he was whisked away into the dark night.

Mrs. Asami returned to her room. She can't remember how she ever lived through that night. She only remembers remaining quiet so as not to waken the sleeping children.

"But I was awake," recalled her eldest, Kinichi, in an interview in Tokyo in 1966. He was 19 in 1941. At the time of the interview, he was vice-chief of the overseas news section of the

46

Kyodo News Service in Tokyo. He said that in 1941 he had been working for his father's paper as a linotype operator to earn enough money to go to college. Kinichi said, "I heard the FBI come to our home. I heard my mother and my father talking. I wanted to get out of my room and see my father, but I stayed in bed. I wanted to talk with my mother, but I didn't. I couldn't sleep. I was worried about the future. Here I was, suddenly thrust into the role as the head of the family."

The eldest daughter, Mrs. Jane Asami Iwashita, was then 16. In an interview in Honolulu in 1966 she remembered "how lost and numb I felt the next morning when I found out my father was gone." She said, "When we heard about the attack on Pearl Harbor on the radio that Sunday morning, my father wouldn't

The Asami family posing for a family picture before sailing on a visit to Japan eighteen months before the war. Front row, *left* to *right,* Jane, Alice, Harold, and Morris. Back row, Mr. and Mrs. Shoichi Asami and Kinichi. *Iwashita Photo Collection.*

Kinichi Asami being interviewed by the author in Tokyo in 1966. *Author's photo collection.*

believe it. A Japanese government official had told him earlier that Japan would never start a war."

Months later, word came from her father from a camp on the mainland that he wanted the family to prepare to leave because they were all going to Japan with him on an exchange ship.

Jane recalled: "We didn't want to go. We wanted to stay in Hawaii. But we felt that to say no would be to forsake him. I felt we owed it to my father to do what he wanted."

Kinichi had felt that way, too. But, using hindsight, he said, "The decision to leave Hawaii was a big mistake. Yes, I made a big mistake. I should have gone against my father's wishes. If only we had objected, I know my father would have stayed in the United States."

As Asami was moved from one camp to another, the rest of the family spent a whole year being shuffled from one hotel to another. "But we were treated really well," said Jane.

Father and family were finally united a year and five months later in May of 1943 in the Crystal City internment camp in Texas. In the fall of 1943 they left aboard the Swedish-American liner *Gripsholm* from New Jersey for the neutral port of exchange in Goa, India. The voyage, by way of South America and Africa, took two months. Jane described the trip as "wonderful . . . comfortable . . . good food and good service."

In contrast, she said, the Japanese *Teia maru,* which they boarded in Goa, was "terrible. The food was terrible. I remember worms floating in the rice. It was overcrowded. Long lines for everything. I can still remember a pregnant woman, nearly ready to give birth. She, too, had to stand in line even to use the toilet. It was pathetic."

When the ship stopped in Singapore, which was captured by Japan in 1942, Japanese officials urged persons who could speak English to get off there because help was needed. Asami, who suffered from asthma, liked the climate in Singapore because it was so much like Hawaii's. So his family, along with twenty others, got off the vessel.

Asami was put to work preparing newspaper dispatches. The two youngest children—Alice, 11, and Harold, 9—went to school. Because there was no intermediate school in Singapore, Morris, 13, was sent to live with Asami's mother in Hikari, a city in Yamaguchi Prefecture in southern Honshu. Jane was put to work monitoring calls of people suspected of being pro-American or pro-British. She said: "I didn't like doing that, but I had no choice."

Kinichi did monitoring too, for a while. Then in October of 1944 he was conscripted into the Japanese army. He said, "I didn't want to go, but if I opposed, I knew I would be put into prison or something. The army was the boss. I could have resisted no matter what the consequences. But I gave in and kept my mouth shut."

Kinichi said it was difficult for him to be in the Japanese army—"a man raised as an American can't become a Japanese soldier just like that. I just didn't have the *bushido* [the way of the samurai] spirit that they did."

While the Japanese soldiers yearned for a bowl of *miso shiru* (soup made of soy bean paste), he was more likely thinking of a Coke or 7-up. For Kinichi, the "biggest ordeal was the strict army discipline. They were really strict."

He trained in Kuala Lumpur and stayed there with the medical corps—away from the front lines—caring for civilian and military tuberculosis patients. Kinichi said he was "very stressed" during the war. "Maybe this was because I was doing something I didn't want to do. I felt pro-American. I was a Hawaiian-American even though my uniform was Japanese. The soldiers treated me regular. Most of them were sympathetic. Some of them asked me about Hawaii. Like me, most of the soldiers worried about their families most of the time. Although we didn't get any word, it was clear which way the war was going from early 1945. We were short of everything—food, supplies, everything."

In March of 1945 the Japanese ordered the civilian evacuation of Singapore because American forces were moving closer and closer. Jane's father arranged for his wife and two daughters to leave by a hospital ship. Passengers included other Japanese civilian families and some prostitutes who had been "stationed" in Singapore.

Asami, 51, and his youngest son Harold, 11, left aboard the *Awa maru,* which was traveling under a U.S. safe conduct pass to supply prison camps holding Allied prisoners of war. As the *Awa maru* moved into waters off the Formosa Strait, a torpedo from an American submarine, the *Queenfish,* exploded into the Japanese vessel. Asami and his son, along with all the other passengers and crew—except one Japanese cook—died with the ship.

Jane said, "It wasn't until we got to Japan that we heard what happened." Years later, after she returned to Hawaii, she read through naval submarine records at the University of Hawaii library and found that the captain of the *Queenfish* was court-martialed for the sinking of the *Awa maru.* She said the records show that the *Queenfish* tried to rescue the people floating in the wreckage. All but one preferred to drown. "I guess that was because the Japanese felt it was a disgrace to be taken prisoner."

In Japan the family moved into her grandmother's shack in Hikari in Honshu. Jane said, "I remember how we hoped against hope that somehow my father and brother had survived, that some miracle had happened. Every time I heard a train come into Hikari, I would jump up to see whether they were on it. For a long while, we refused to believe that they had died."

When Kinichi learned of the tragedy, he said he cried inwardly in utter frustration because he was helpless to do anything for his family. His worries expressed themselves in a recurring dream in which his mother toiled in the fields in rags. But the Asamis in Hikari had no time to grieve. They were quickly put to work.

Morris, the brother who had come to Hikari earlier, worked in a naval arsenal with other students. The arsenal was a branch of the suicide corps and part of the work was building suicide torpedoes. Mrs. Asami worked in the neighborhood corps. Her job was to plant vegetables and to gather pine branches from which oil was extracted. Even young Alice, 13, was put to work in school. Because Jane could speak English, she was assigned to the library at the arsenal. "But," she laughed, "I wasn't much help because all the books were in German." She was paid about 60 yen a month, but "money was worthless because there was nothing in the stores to buy."

She said the daylight air raids were persistent. "We spent most of our time running up into the mountains or into tunnels drilled through the mountains." The raids also took place nightly at eleven o'clock. "Toward the end of the war, we didn't even bother going to the shelters," Jane said. "We were so tired."

More than the raids, the problem that plagued Jane was relations with the people in Hikari. "I really had a miserable time," she said. "I was never accepted. No matter how hard I tried to look Japanese, I just looked different, I guess. The factory workers would heckle me. They threw stones and sticks and

Jane Asami in her formal wear, c. 1946. *Iwashita Photo Collection.*

called me names, like 'foreign dog', 'American spy', and even 'General MacArthur's mistress' after the war."

"Also, because permanent waves were banned to conserve energy, I used to pull my curly hair into a pony tail or pigtails. But the curls eventually showed and the heckling would start all over again. I felt like yelling at them, but I knew that would only make things worse." There was a catch in her throat of uncried tears as she recalled the agony of the harassment on her long walk to and from work.

She said, "I was very bitter at the way they were treating me. But today I realize their behavior toward me wasn't really their fault. The Japanese were brainwashed to be unquestionably loyal—ultranationalistic. They were incapable of doing their own thinking. And the propaganda about the Americans was horrible. They were told that if Japan lost, all the men would be sold as slaves and all the women would be raped. The adults swallowed all that. But the younger children were honestly curious in the way that children can be. They would come up to me secretly and ask 'Are the Americans really mean? Would they rape me?' I would assure them that Americans weren't like that."

As it was with Kinichi in Kuala Lumpur, Jane remembers the constant concern over food. A good part of each day her family scoured the hills for something edible—roots, nuts, wild greens. Their diet consisted mostly of a little rice mixed with tasteless *daizu* (soybean) from which the oil had been squeezed out, and sweet potatoes, or fish caught in polluted waters.

Jane said, "We didn't starve, but there was never enough food, however horrible. I saw how evil people can become when there's not enough to eat. Then there was the stealing, plotting, and deceptions. Over and over," she said, "I would daydream about the end of the war and our return home to Hawaii."

The end of the war finally did come, but not before the arsenal was the victim of a direct hit—and, the awesome Hiroshima A-bombing.

Jane said, "It was just luck that my brother Morris was on the night shift when the arsenal was bombed one day. A lot of young students were killed. It was so pitiful." She remembered the flood of rumors that erupted out of the Hiroshima bombing. Some called it the "death ray bomb" and said that to see even the flash of the bomb meant certain death. She saw one of the bomb victims who had come all the way to Hikari to get help from her uncle, a doctor. She shuddered at the memory: "The man died shortly after he reached Hikari. I remember the horrible blisters on the soles of his feet. There were maggots in the blisters."

She spent the last day of the war in the mountains, where she fled to escape an air raid in the city. The terror of the arsenal bombing the day before was still so vivid in her mind. She stayed in the mountains until nightfall.

She was overjoyed to learn when she returned home that the emperor had announced the surrender. Jane's mother said his voice was soft. That was the first time the emperor had ever spoken to his people. He had said that it was best to surrender because he didn't want his nation to suffer anymore.

"I was so happy," Jane said, "I just couldn't tell you how happy."

Kinichi, too, heard the emperor's radio address in his army barracks in Kuala Lumpur. He said, "I was really happy. I had kept hoping for the end. But I couldn't say that openly. After the emperor spoke, some of the soldiers cried. Most of them were quiet and worried about the future. One officer committed suicide." Kinichi had to remain in Kuala Lumpur for two years to act as an interpreter for the British. He didn't get to Japan until 1947.

In Hikari the end of the war did not bring wondrous overnight changes, either, for Jane and the rest of the family. Jane said, "Food was still scarce. I still worked at the arsenal, mostly cleaning up. There were dead bodies all over. The stench was overpowering. One thing that still amazes me is that the old people were talking about how there was still a chance to win, despite all the signs of defeat around them. They got bamboo spears ready to 'attack the Americans' when word would be given for an all-out fight on the homefront. They just refused to believe that Japan had lost. They said it was a lie."

While her brother interpreted for the British, Jane's command of English was used by arsenal officials to prepare an inventory of all property to be turned over to the Americans. Later she worked for a colonel with the American occupation forces, "but I quit when I found out he wanted me to be his mistress. The Americans were kind of 'wild' in some cases. I guess a lot of them had come right from battle. Some soldiers tried to bribe the girls with 'state-side candy' and 'state-side lipstick'. Those were unstable days and a lot of war babies were born as a result."

It took Jane a while to find a job "where I'd be respected for myself with no strings attached." She found one with the U.S. Counter Intelligence Corps. She earned 3,000 yen a month

Jane Asami working as a translator-interpreter for the U.S. Counter Intelligence Corps after the war. *Iwashita Photo Collection.*

(about $200 in 1945–1946) doing translating. For the first time in years, she recalled, "I had one good meal a day. The Americans I worked with knew how tough things were for us and shared their rations with me—a piece of meat, canned goods and sweets. I remember my first Hershey bar. It tasted soooo good. And I remember my first pair of postwar shoes and underwear and American soap—with suds—and toilet paper and sanitary pads. Oh, it was such a joy."

All the while, Jane kept her sights on "my goal to regain my U.S. citizenship, which I had lost the moment I got on the exchange ship to Japan." Because she had worked for the enemy government, the legal road back to becoming a U.S. citizen was rocky, but she finally got her passport back to Hawaii.

"I can't begin to tell you how happy I was," she said. "I cherish my citizenship very much. I'm proud to be an American and proud that America is my home. But, you know, the war taught me that I must be a citizen of the world first, and a citizen of the United States second. I began thinking that way when I saw how dangerous ultranationalism can be—as it was in Japan."

Jane was 22, and her sister, Alice, 15, when they returned to Hawaii in 1947. They were followed shortly afterward by Morris, 17, and then later by Mrs. Asami. The family learned that Mr. Asami's friends and former newspaper colleagues had held a memorial service for him and his son, Harold, on December 23, 1945, in Honolulu. Program notes for the service state that Asami, originally from Yamaguchi Prefecture, arrived in Hawaii in 1913 at age 19. His parents were already in the Islands. Asami, who had been with a news service in Japan, first worked with a magazine in Hilo on the Big Island before joining the editorial staff of the *Nippu jiji* in 1916. He served as an editor of the Japanese language section of the bilingual newspaper until he was picked up by the FBI.

Jane said the family home in Kaimuki had been confiscated by the U.S. government. With the help of relatives and friends, the Asamis regrouped to begin life in Hawaii again. Jane worked as a maid for the Spaldings on Makiki Heights. She and Morris went through the University of Hawaii working part-time.

Jane said, "My brother [Morris] felt like a misfit throughout the war. I think he began to feel comfortable once he settled into his job as a U.S. customs examiner in Los Angeles." Her sister Alice attended McKinley High School and later got married and moved to Los Angeles.

Jane also married. Toraki Terry Iwashita was an engineer with the submarine unit at Pearl Harbor. They had three children. Eventually Jane got a teaching degree and worked with youngsters with severe reading problems or who were emotionally disturbed.

Because of his Japanese army service, Kinichi said, "I resigned myself to settling in Japan, even though deep down I will always be Hawaiian first, Japanese second." He visited Hawaii for the first time in twenty-four years in 1965 and was amazed at the changes and at the remaining warm bond of friendship with old friends. He said, "I had a lump in my throat when I went to see the two houses we used to live in in Kaimuki. It wasn't easy to see other people living there."

One of the cherished mementos Mr. Asami left for his family is a book of Japanese poetry, *Kaicho On* (Sounds of the Ocean Tides), he wrote and had published in 1922 to commemorate his marriage. Ironically, he stated in one of his poems that should he have the choice, he would wish "to be taken by the fury of the waves."

———————◼———————
# 1990 Update

Jane Michiko Asami Iwashita died of cancer at age 57 in Honolulu in 1981. A few moments after her death, her mother, Mrs. Shizu Asami, closed her daughter's eyes and said tenderly, *"Mit-chan, yokatta, ne?* [Mit-chan, it all worked out well, didn't it?]."

Jane's eldest daughter Teresa said, "My mother and grandmother were so close. You know, after all that they had gone through together, they were never bitter." Mrs. Asami died in Honolulu in 1984 at age 86.

Her eldest son, Kinichi, 68, is still a vice-chief of the overseas news section of the Kyodo News Service in Tokyo. He continues to hope that he and his wife may someday live in Hawaii. They have two children, one of whom, Kumiko Nii, is living in Honolulu while her husband, a businessman, is assigned there.

Morris, 60, has retired from the U.S. Customs Service in California. He is married and lives in Torrance.

Alice Asami Niiya, 58, also lives in Torrance with her husband. They have a son.

In addition to Teresa, 38, Jane is survived by her son, Calvin, 34, and daughter, Amy, 30.

Teresa said that before her mother died, she talked a lot about the family's wartime experiences. "Someday," Teresa said, "I hope to write their story."

# Chapter 3

# THE TANAKA STORY

In the quiet of a gray November morning in Honolulu, Mrs. Haru Tanaka, 74, of Wahiawa remembered Pearl Harbor and a flood of other World War II remembrances in this way:

"*Ureshii koto* [Happy times].

"*Osoroshii koto* [Frightening times].

"*Kanashii koto* [Sad times].

"*Kangai muryo* [I remember with deep emotions].

"*Naitemo, naitemo tamaranai* [Overwhelming beyond tears]."

She closed her eyes for a moment as if to clear out the flood of memories that crisscrossed her mind. She sat up erect, her hands folded in her lap, as she remembered a moment of searing intensity one long ago day in 1943 in an alien internment camp in Crystal City, Texas. She closed her eyes again as if to relive that moment in her mind as she spoke: "My fingers trembled as I tore open the envelope bordered in red, white, and blue. It was a letter from my only son—Akira. It was a letter from home— Hawaii. I got a trifle angry at myself when the tears started and blurred my spectacles. I wiped them off impatiently.

"The letter began: 'Mom' . . . Akira apologized for not writing sooner and hoped I was being treated well in the camp. Abruptly, I stiffened when I read: 'I've volunteered to be in the American Army. I am now an American soldier. I must fight, and if necessary, I must die for my country.' I froze. I stared at the barbed wire that held me in this alien camp. I felt anxious as I thought to myself: 'I may never see him again.' I felt so helpless.

"How I wished I could see Akira once more. And then, I felt such a deep sadness. Even now, years later, the memory of that episode chills me." She massaged her hands as if she were cold as she continued.

"I looked deep into myself that day. I told myself: 'You're a Japanese national. But, Akira is an American citizen.' I remembered how often I had taught him to be a good American . . . to do his duty for his country.

"In the quiet of my heart, I was very proud of him. Akira had learned well. I was proud that he had volunteered. I was proud that he had measured up, that he was willing to die for his country. I was proud that he was, indeed, a good American."

Mrs. Tanaka thought a long moment and then continued: "Akira's letter jarred me at first because of all that had happened to me after Japan bombed Pearl Harbor that Sunday morning. I was shocked that day. And terribly worried. My daughter [Muriel Chiyo] had been in Tokyo since 1939 studying at the Women's Art College. What would happen to her now? When I saw the planes that morning, I thought they were training with make-believe enemy planes with red Rising Sun emblems painted on them. Then, someone yelled out: '*Senso! Senso!* [War! War!].'

"I saw a plane fall nearby and burn two houses. Fire started in a third. One of the families had been asleep and ran out in nightclothes. A woman had just come back from buying bread when she saw her house burst into flames. There was a lot of *gujaguja* [confusion] as people rushed to help."

She took a deep breath before she went on: "Early that afternoon, four FBI men came to my house. They pointed their guns at me. 'Change clothes! Change clothes!' they ordered. I was frightened. They followed my every move, even to the bathroom. I was not allowed to take anything more than the clothes on my back. They let me leave a note for Akira, who was out on a National Guard training exercise."

She was taken because she had been the principal of the Showa Japanese Language School in Wahiawa after her husband died in 1928, shortly after he founded the school. The school held classes in language and culture, including Japanese sewing and the martial arts. She had also helped as a community liaison for the Japanese Consulate.

She was taken to the immigration station in Honolulu at midnight, after the FBI men picked up other Japanese language teachers and Buddhist priests. They stayed there for two months and were then transferred to a camp on Sand Island in Honolulu. "Most of that time," she said, "we had no change of clothes. Nightly, we rinsed our things out and dried them under our bunks. Later, our friends were allowed to send us some clothes."

Then one day the detainees got individual orders from the U.S. government that they were to be moved to mainland camps. "Several alien German women with us wailed and cried," she said. "Because none of the Japanese internees cried, one of the German women asked if we were going to be released. I told her that we, too, had gotten the same order and that we, too, cry. Inwardly. 'Japanese don't show tears outwardly,'" I explained.

A few months later, her group was shipped out on the SS *Lurline* to a girls' reformatory school in Dallas, Texas, which had been converted into an internment center. They stayed there for a year with Japanese internees from Peru before moving to a camp in Crystal City, Texas. They received thirty-five cents a day for personal purchases at the camp store.

Mrs. Tanaka recalled: "It was a terrible place, with snakes, scorpions, and a lot of other creatures of the desert. It was so hot and then it was so cold. And the dry dust blew everywhere and got into everything. The days dragged—one upon the other. We had no contact with the outside world, except letters from friends and relatives. I told myself, 'I can spend each day in worry and in bitterness. Or I can spend each day being useful and hopeful.' For me, it was a choice between life and death. And I was not ready for death."

Mrs. Tanaka and the others started up a group of language,

art, and craft classes for youngsters and adults. She headed a class for some two hundred students, including nisei wanting to learn Japanese before they left for Japan under war exchange programs. She taught Japanese Sunday School and held arts and crafts classes for teenagers. She was paid $13 a month for teaching.

She, herself, took a correspondence course in English so she could write to Akira, because letters written in Japanese were not permitted through the mail during the war. To this day she practices writing in English.

The women were happy because they could do their own cooking, a source of much pleasure. Crystal City was one of the few family-oriented camps with a population of some 3,500 Japanese. Mrs. Tanaka recalled how they had improvised to cope with food rationing and the lack of Japanese seasoning. She chuckled as she told how they had used black, left-over coffee, salt, and sugar to make a kind of teriyaki (barbecue) sauce without shoyu.

While camp life had its enjoyable moments, it was far from being like home. The days became months and the months faded into years. The longest hours for Mrs. Tanaka were those before sleep would come when she worried about Muriel and Akira.

For Akira, however, the days flipped by rapidly, rapidly.

Immediately after the nightmare of Pearl Harbor and his mother's forced departure, Akira joined the new Hawaii Territorial Guard with other University of Hawaii students. In an interview in 1966 Akira said he had felt upset when the nisei boys were pulled out of the guard because their loyalty was questioned. But, Akira said, "I had no hard feelings, because such were the times."

He went back to the university and worked nights in the Office of Civilian Defense until the nisei were allowed to become American soldiers in March 1943. He volunteered for the 442nd Regimental Combat Team, but didn't get selected until the second nisei unit, an intelligence group, was formed.

He said simply: "I volunteered because it was my duty to my country."

Unlike the 442nd boys who trained for the European campaign at Camp Shelby, Mississippi, Akira's group trained at Camp Savage, Minnesota, to become Japanese interpreters and translators in the Pacific War. He said, "We got our first practice session interrogating Japanese prisoners at a POW camp in Hawaii, near Ewa. We didn't have any trouble. The prisoners were friendly. I guess they depended on us to receive good treatment. One of the prisoners was a Farrington High School graduate [Isamu Shimogawa, class of 1939]. He had been stranded in Japan when the war started. I couldn't help wondering whether my sister, too, was a prisoner somewhere."

Then came the landing on Leyte in October 1944, followed by the Okinawa campaign. Akira said, "We interpreters moved with the fighting units, but we were behind the front lines. Behind, but not too far behind."

While Akira sloshed through the jungles of the Pacific, his sister Muriel was in Tokyo tracking movements of American forces for Japanese intelligence through long- and short-wave radio monitoring. She, like other dual citizens, had been conscripted to work for the Japanese government a few months after that day in December 1941 when she had awakened to the blare of Japanese military marches and proud announcements of American ships sunk at Pearl Harbor.

Muriel, also interviewed in 1966, said rumors of war floated about in the months preceding the attack, "but I didn't believe them and made no effort to return home to Hawaii." She and other bilingual nisei were highly sought after for communications work. Most Japanese women worked in war factories.

Muriel was assigned to monitor ABC, BBC, and other radio broadcasts and communiques from Allied commands in the Pacific telling about bombing missions. She said, "The figures were always exaggerated because it was understood that these communiques were being monitored. I guess this kind of thing was done on both sides."

Through this kind of electronic eavesdropping, both sides heard about troop movements. During the long intervals between communiques, Muriel said she got to hear the latest American pop music, like Frank Sinatra's "Paper Doll" and Glenn Miller's "Moonlight Serenade."

She worked in the same building housing the supreme command for the Japanese military forces. Leaders, such as Premier Hideki Tojo, had their headquarters in the building. She said, "I occasionally saw Tojo coming into the building amid a lot of fanfare. He was always stern-faced. Once a year we used to see the emperor too. He made an annual visit to the command and we all bowed as he passed. On those occasions, we got special box lunches filled with good things to eat that we never could get the rest of the year. And there were special cakes too. Little round cakes shaped like the Imperial family's chrysanthemum emblem. Inside the cakes was a lot of the black sugar that I longed for."

Muriel was the highest paid woman worker on the nine-woman staff. She earned 81 yen a month which covered her basic needs well. She said, "I blanked out thoughts of home. I didn't think I could live through the war. I felt under constant duress and survived from day to day, doing what I had to do.

"American B-29s bombed Tokyo now and then even early in the war. Later, American planes came every noon and night. We used to say: 'There goes B-chan again. [*Chan* is a Japanese suffix of affection, like Amy-chan.]'

"The planes flew so high that Japanese antiaircraft guns couldn't even reach them. The bombings got heavier and more frequent toward the end of the war. I'll never forget all the running I did to escape the bombs, with a tea kettle for boiling water and cooking stuffed in my bag. It was amazing how accurate the hits were at times. I remember once when bombs burst on all sides of the general headquarters.

"One night in 1944, incendiary 'jelly' bombs burned all the buildings in our compound except the one I was sleeping in. I guess they're called 'jelly' because the material stuck to the skin and burned."

Muriel said, "My heart ached for my mother when I saw her name on a Red Cross roster of aliens interned in the United States. I just sat there and wept. I received two letters from my mother during the war. One came through the prisoner-of-war mail system and another through the Red Cross. Both letters were heavily censored."

Because Muriel worked for the military, food rations were provided. Her diet included rice mixed with grain, dried fish, noodles, sweet potatoes, pumpkin, turnip, and even weeds. Once in a rare while lumps of brown sugar came from Okinawa. Otherwise, it was saccharin "and I never want to eat that again."

As a result of the starch-laden diet, she came down with beri-beri. Her main symptom was constant fatigue. Fortunately, she had a doctor-friend who gave her medication to treat the disease.

She worked a twelve-hour shift and at night she spent time sifting the rice from the mixture of bad-tasting grain. "We'd sit there picking rice grains out one by one."

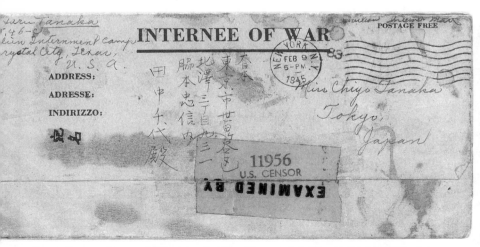

One of two pieces of "Detained Alien Enemy Mail" received by Muriel Chiyo Tanaka (now Onishi) from her interned mother during the war. *Tanaka Collection.*

As an occasional treat they played bridge in the near darkness. Strict blackout and smoke restrictions, she said, forbade the burning of coal or wood during the cold winter months. Besides, coal was scarce.

Muriel remembered "how careful I had to be to look 'native' because some of the people were quite nasty toward nisei. I dyed my old saddle oxfords and loafers black because their styling was a dead American giveaway. My two pairs of shoes lasted me through the war with frequent repairs done with old rubber tire patches. My hair was a mess in those days. I wore pigtails because beauty shops were closed to save electricity, and the metal used for curlers and equipment was melted down for the war effort.

"All the women wore drab *mompei*s [bloomerlike pants]. These were cut out from kimonos. The top of the kimono was cut to become a blouse. The full sleeves were chopped off to fit like shirt sleeves. The lower part of the kimono was made into *mompei*s snapped at the ankles and sashed at the waist."

As Japan began to feel the crushing wallop of U.S. might, Muriel and the others in the communications sector were evacuated to a large home in a suburb of Tokyo to continue their monitoring. Muriel said: "I knew the end was inevitable, especially after the Americans took Truk and Midway. The Japanese officers were hot on our necks all the time to find out what we had picked up. 'What did they say? What did they say?' they kept asking us."

Then came the destruction of Hiroshima on August 6, 1945, and of Nagasaki on August 8.

Muriel said, "Word of the A-bomb attacks spread like the radiation itself. No one knew what the bomb was, but they knew it was a new devastating force. There was so much fear. Some people referred to the bomb as *obake* [devil]. Mostly, it was called *pika-don,* a descriptive phrase referring to the sudden flash [*pika*] and the noise [*don*].

"People from all over rushed to Hiroshima to search for the bodies of relatives and got severely sick from the exposure. My

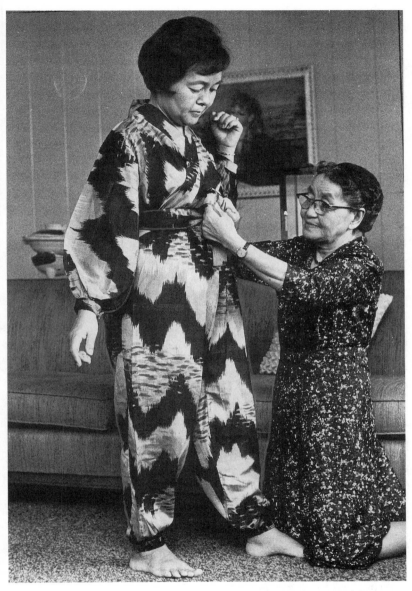

Haru Tanaka getting her daughter, Muriel Onishi, ready to model a *mom-pei*. *Star-Bulletin Photo by the late Al Yamauchi.*

Akira Tanaka and his sister Muriel happily reunited in 1945 in the Japanese countryside. *Tanaka Photo Collection.*

uncle was one of them. He was the former mayor of Etajima, an island off Hiroshima. He searched through the ashes for his son who had died in the bombing. The exposure to the radiation is gradually disintegrating my uncle's internal organs."

She said, "The rumor after the Nagasaki bombing was that the next explosion would be in Tokyo on the morning of August 9. We were really frightened. August 9 came and went with no bombs. What a relief!"

Muriel recalled the emperor's announcement of surrender on August 15: "We just cried. It was a cry of relief. Sadness, too, and anxiety over the uncertain future. We just let go emotionally after all those years—day and night—under constant tension. We were constantly under surveillance at work and after work." After the emperor's "endure the unendurable" speech, she said, "even the officers were relieved. I could tell. But for some, the surrender was too much. They committed suicide. We saw young soldiers, too, committing suicide because they felt so disgraced.

"I guess they felt that was the only honorable thing they could do because, in their way of thinking, they had failed their emperor and their country—their very reason for existence."

She said officials apparently thought America would attack by land because "before the end came, women were warned to stay out of sight when the Americans came. They said the Americans would rape all the women."

After the surrender Muriel served as an interpreter for the influx of Americans traveling on the Tokyo-Yokohama railway express trains. She later worked as a foreign national for the U.S. Civil Information and Education Section of the Occupation forces, doing cultural research and office tasks.

She recalled a startling November night in 1945: "It was midnight. There was heavy pounding on my door. When I opened it, my heart jumped. There, silhouetted in the doorway were three American GIs. I was terrified. And then, one of them called my name. It was my brother, Akira, with two of his friends. I was really happy to see him. It was a big relief to hear that he had seen my mother at her camp."

Akira returned to Hawaii in 1946 after serving for a year with the Occupation forces in Seoul, Korea. He went back to the University of Hawaii and transferred later to Michigan State University. When he was interviewed in 1966 he was head of one of the design departments of the Chevrolet division of General Motors in Detroit. He is married to the former Judith Doue of Honolulu. They have two children.

Muriel's return to Hawaii was delayed until 1947. She had lost her U.S. citizenship at the end of the war because of her work for the Japanese government. For the two years her case was under investigation, she was a person without a country.

She, along with nineteen other nisei who regained their citizenship at the same time, returned aboard the *General Gordon*. Muriel said, "I had the best food in years aboard the ship." She said her mother's first words upon her return were: " 'Yokatta. Yokatta. [How good that everything turned out so well.]' "

Muriel said, "My first Thanksgiving at home was so meaningful. I was so grateful to have survived the war and then to return home safely and to have our family together again."

In 1948 she married Harold Onishi, whom she had met while he served with the Occupation forces. Muriel, mother of two children, teaches summers at the Honolulu Academy of Arts and devotes many hours to Girl Scout and Harris United Methodist Church activities.

She said, "Each December 7th, I am fully aware what day it is. And I say to myself, 'Thank goodness it's over.' I get chills as I remember the blare of military music that woke me up at 6 A.M. that December morning in Tokyo." She said, "I was spared in the war. I feel I was spared for a purpose. I try to fulfill this in a sense through my church and community work."

She said, "There's no place like Hawaii. And yet, I have a yearning to see the people in Tokyo again. I suffered with the people there in so many ways. I saw the best and the worst in them during those years. There was a bond that was established between us that I cannot deny. My heart will always be torn in two parts—Hawaii and Tokyo."

For Muriel's mother, the end of the war was "bittersweet." Mrs. Tanaka said, "The end came unexpectedly. Because there was no free communication with the world outside the camp, we didn't know what was happening. When camp officials told us that Japan had surrendered, I didn't know whether to be happy or sad. I was just relieved it was all over. But I was sad that Japan had to be the loser. Of course, I realized that in a war, one side loses and one side wins. Many people in the camp said the surrender was a lie. I was just glad it was over."

Mrs. Tanaka remained in the internment camp for another four months because returning ships were crowded. When she finally came back to Hawaii, she recalled: "It was a sad and lonely homecoming. My house was confiscated. The school was sold." She stayed with friends in Wahiawa for a while. Then she started up private flower arrangement, art, cooking, and sewing classes in her home to begin her long, hard climb back to stand on her own two feet again.

In 1966, at a spunky 74, she still served as a vice-principal of the Wahiawa Japanese Language School. That year, the Japanese community honored her for her forty-nine years of teaching service.

Mrs. Tanaka refuses to dwell on the war years. She said, "The fact that the three of us pulled through the war makes up for all the lost years and all the loss of material belongings."

In 1955 she did "the only thing I could do to express my feelings to America. I became a naturalized American citizen." She said, "Both of my children are Americans. I live on American soil. During my internment, the Americans were generous and treated us well. America has been good to me. I owe a lot to this country. I want to serve America. This is my home; this is my country."

This is why she said, "*Naitemo, naitemo tamaranai* [Overwhelming beyond tears]."

■

# 1990 Update

At 97, Mrs. Haru Tanaka still lives by herself in a cottage in Wahiawa, her home base since 1925, except for the four years she was interned. She retired in 1982 after more than sixty years of teaching and serving as the principal of the Wahiawa Japanese Language School. She joins her friends at the Wahiawa Senior Center each day for singing, arts and crafts, outings, and lunch.

And each Saturday afternoon she takes the bus into downtown Honolulu to visit her daughter and son-in-law, Muriel and Harold M. Onishi. If they're not at the bus stop when she arrives, she starts walking. The Onishis live a good forty-five-minute walk away. She's just as precise about returning to Wahiawa. Despite pleas that she stay through Sunday night, she insists on taking the bus back right after Sunday morning service at Harris United Methodist Church because she feels her friends are counting on her to be there on Monday morning.

Mrs. Tanaka attributes her long and active life to the Nishi Health System developed in Japan. It has the earmarks of today's New Age health programs that emphasize exercise, diet, and internal cleansing—except that she has been a Nishi disciple since the 1930s.

Curiously, her diet is not all grain, vegetables, and tofu. She eats whatever she pleases, including beef, pork, and chicken. She prefers those to fish, having had her fill of fish as a youngster in Japan. What's more, she has an enormous sweet tooth. Says her daughter, "You should see her grocery cart, filled with cookies, pies, cakes, and ice cream."

As one of Hawaii's oldest surviving Japanese internees of World War II, Mrs. Tanaka was among the first group to receive the $20,000 in reparations from the U.S. government in October 1990. She will donate her money to charitable organizations.

Mrs. Haru Tanaka flashes a big smile following redress ceremonies in October 1990. To her *right* is her daughter Muriel. *Tanaka Photo Collection.*

The Onishis are hoping to have Mrs. Tanaka move in with them next year because she is getting very forgetful and isn't the housekeeper she used to be. She will be 98 on March 29, 1991.

Her daughter says, "She's such a legend in Wahiawa. Everyone knows her there as Tanaka-*sensei* (teacher)—the strict teacher that her ex-students all say really taught them something." She has received many tributes from her former students, as well as from the community and the Japanese government.

Muriel Onishi, too, is in active retirement at 69 with her husband Harold. Since retiring as office manager for the Girl Scouts of Hawaii in 1986, she has been volunteering more time to church activities. The Onishis have a son and a daughter.

Two years ago, Mrs. Onishi visited Japan for the first time in forty-one years. "I was overcome," she said, "I really felt like a foreigner in a new country. So crowded. So many towering buildings and fast-food American places in Tokyo. I was amazed to see everyone so well dressed—not the way I remember Japan in 1947. I'm happy for the Japanese for such a remarkable recovery."

She went to her old Women's Art College and found her name listed in the alumni section. "It was like finding a part of me, a validation of a part of my past," she said.

Her brother, Akira Tanaka, 67, is recognized for his inventions in the auto safety world. As an inventor-engineer for General Motors, he created one of the first seat belts in the United States. He also developed the luxury car seat that can be height-regulated. He was a consultant with the American Safety Company on vehicular safety devices, and later opened his own plastic molding company in Encino, California.

# Chapter 4

•

# THE YEMPUKU STORY

The hillside house on the tiny island of Atatashima in Japan's Inland Sea was as still as a silk-screen painting. Occasionally, sounds from the fishing boats below wafted up. Occasionally, the wind played on the *shoji* doors in the elegantly simple house.

Mrs. Gofuyo Yempuku, 76, drank in the view—the velvet mountains to the right and the shimmering Inland Sea to the left. And far beyond, Hiroshima City. As if content that nothing had changed since she last looked, she folded herself onto a blue and white *zabuton* (cushion). She looked as fragile as her floral arrangement nearby. But fragile she was not during the interview at her home in 1966 when she opened the doors to memories that, she confided, were of a painful period.

"When we heard the news about Pearl Harbor," she said, "we were here in Atatashima. We felt so torn. We love Hawaii and we love this country. My husband and I spent twenty-five good years in Hawaii in the small plantation town of Kahuku and it was not easy to forget twenty-five good years. He went there to serve as a Buddhist priest and I taught at the Japanese language school in Kahuku.

"We knew Tsuneto [Ralph], the oldest of our five sons, would be in the U.S. Army because he was the right age. He was the only member of the family who stayed in Hawaii when we left in 1933. Then, our boys here went off to fight. And even our youngest son [Paul] was put to work in a war plant. It tore our hearts knowing that our sons were fighting against each other.

75

The Yempukus' last family portrait before all but Ralph, the eldest son, left for Atatashima, Japan, in 1933. Front row, Mr. and Mrs. Yempuku and Paul. Back, *left* to *right,* Toru, Donald, Ralph, and Goro. *Yempuku Photo Collection.*

"*Shikata ga nai* [It couldn't be helped].
"*Akiramemashita* [We accepted the fate].
"I was so relieved at the way things turned out."

Mrs. Yempuku shook her head of lovely white hair, loosely pulled into a tiny bun in the back. She said, "When the war ended, it was no surprise to us that America won. We had forecast that long before. We knew America. We knew she was rich and strong. We knew it would be a tough, tough struggle for Japan. But we couldn't talk about this with others because we feared possible police action. We knew defeat would come to Japan," she said. "Japan could never win against the United States, we used to tell each other."

She went on: "It was terribly lonesome here. My husband

and I alone in this house. And there was so little food. We ate grain mixed in our rice that was normally fed to cattle and horses. People were sick constantly. *Kuroo shimashita* [We went through much suffering]."

She said the people on the island were not unfriendly toward them although they knew that the Yempukus had lived in Hawaii for a long time.

Mrs. Yempuku, bundled in a gray kimono and jacket, rose and surveyed the majestic scene spread before her. She pointed toward Hiroshima City miles away and recalled: "When the atomic bomb fell on August 6, 1945, I could see white smoke over the city. I saw the flash even from here, but I didn't hear any sound. I was in the kitchen cooking. I couldn't imagine what it was all about. I wondered about it all day. Later that evening, my younger brother, who had been in the city, told us about the horror—the destruction and death throughout the city. He had gone to look for his daughter and never found her. He died from radiation sickness.

"Then came the surrender. What a tremendous relief that was. Ralph came here soon after that. *Bikkuri shimashita* [I was really startled]. We thought he had died. There were all sorts of rumors about nisei soldiers being used as first wave combat troops. We were told that thousands of nisei soldiers were dying because of that. So you can imagine what a surprise it was to see him."

She dabbed her eyes and then added, "Ralph had come at night. He had his American uniform on. The people in the area were talking about killing him. He was the enemy. They had been told Americans were cruel and mean. Many of them had lost their loved ones. One family lost three children. They didn't know Ralph was my son. Only later did they know that."

She said, "I was happy my husband had lived through the hard times to see all of his sons again. They returned one by one. And then within a year, Goro took over the priesthood in our family temple here on Atatashima. So, my husband was at peace when he died in 1952."

Captain Ralph Yempuku with the U.S. Counter Intelligence Corps in Japan, 1945. *Yempuku Photo Collection.*

"When I build up my strength," she said, "I dream of going to Hawaii once more. To go there and see my old friends, our old neighborhood. That would be such a pleasure." She turned her gaze again to the mountains and the sea.

Of the five Yempuku brothers, Toru is the "quiet one." "He's always been very reserved," family members say. And Toru, as it turned out, didn't step out of character during his interview in Atatashima in 1966. He answered all questions put to him quickly, quietly, and briefly. No more, no less.

He was in high school when the family moved to Japan and he was in college in Osaka when the war started. He was drafted into the Japanese army a year later because "you couldn't say no when they called you. You either got in or got shot or ended up in prison. There was no choice." At first he served in Japan and then later was sent to fight in Central and South China. He described his feeling during the war as "not pro-American or pro-Japan. I just went with the tide. I didn't let myself think about much."

The end of the war found Toru in a prisoner of war camp in Shanghai and it wasn't until the summer of 1946 that he was released to return to Japan.

While army discipline was "really tough" throughout the war, he said, "I was treated well after the surrender because I could speak English." Toru said he was "not exactly happy or sad" over Japan's surrender—"just relieved, because in China, too, there wasn't enough food to go around." But, he pointed out, "I did feel that I am Japanese and this is where I ought to stay."

After the war, he took on various jobs, primarily as an interpreter. In 1966 he was working as a document translator for the U.S. Military Assistance–Advisory Group in Tokyo.

He said, "I miss Hawaii at times. I'd like to see my old friends again, but it's difficult. I have a family now and we have no plans to leave Japan. I remember a lot of things about Hawaii. Sometimes it doesn't seem real that I was there once. It's so long ago."

Goro is the gentle Yempuku. Not gentleness bred of softness, but gentleness bred of inner strength. For it was Goro who yielded youth's restless spirit and, instead, remained in Atatashima's tiny world to carry on the priestly tradition that belonged to his father and his father's father before him. Like his mother, and certainly his father, Goro is terribly fond of the secluded island and its people—especially the youngsters.

In addition to serving as the priest for the community's Buddhist population of some six hundred, Goro also teaches at the village school.

During the interview in 1966, Goro radiated enthusiasm as he spoke of the "great changes" that have come about for youngsters with Japan's crushing World War II defeat and the advent of democracy that followed in Japan. "You can see the changes best in the students," he said. "Their eyes have been opened. Their vision has been broadened. Now, they see the world, instead of the narrow focus on Japan that used to exist. Previously, education in Japan was keyed to nationalism. There was very little concern about the rest of the world. And the little there was was derogatory. Now, we teach the children to look at the good and the bad of Japan; the good and the bad of other countries. The result is that rather than supernationalism, education is breeding curiosity about the world—about what goes on around them."

Goro beamed. "It is such a change. In the past, children were forbidden to speak up. Today, we encourage them to express themselves. To me, *minshu-shugi* [democracy], unlike *gunkoku* [military rule], enables human beings to be more responsible, more accountable by giving them the right to make their own decisions, rather than being forced to accept decisions made by the military rulers.

"Democracy has been good for Japan," he said, and admitted, "I didn't feel that way at all in the confusing days of 1945." Goro said, "I felt badly when Japan lost the war, but it was a consolation that it was America that we had lost to. It's hard to describe my feelings then. I had mixed emotions. I left Hawaii when I was still in grade school. When the war came, I was 16, and most of my life had been spent in Japan. I felt loyal to Japan. That's the way I felt when I was conscripted into the army.

"And yet," he said, "all the while, there was this gnawing feeling about my older brother Ralph being in Hawaii, in America. He was there and I was here. We were banging heads. This created odd feelings. I can't put them into words."

Goro served in the army in Hiroshima City and then in Kyushu. He didn't hear about the atomic bomb until well after the surrender because he was in Kyushu. He said, "We were just told that America had introduced a new type of bomb and were advised to carry blankets to cover ourselves when enemy planes came.

"While defeat was hard to take, I was greatly relieved when the war ended. Because of all that they went through, Japanese, today, cherish peace intensely."

Goro returned again to the subject closest to his heart: "It's such a satisfaction to see the youngsters graduate from our village elementary school and then make their way to the big schools in Hiroshima City. But it's sad, too, to see them leave when they outgrow our island and migrate to bigger towns."

There was a touch of anxiety in his voice as he noted, "My three children will also outgrow this island some day. And once again, a decision will have to be made—who will carry on where I leave off?" Nostalgically, he added, "Before I die, I hope I can go back to Kahuku in Hawaii and see my birthplace once more."

Paul, the youngest of the Yempukus, was 6 when he left Hawaii for Japan. He was 14 when the war began. He vividly remembers the day: "Our class was helping to build a sports center in Hiroshima City. We were carrying sand when we heard the Japanese Navy song over the loudspeakers: '*Mamoru mo semeru mo kuni no tame* . . . [Defend and attack for our country].' Then, somebody announced that Japan had bombed Pearl Harbor." Paul said, "Although I knew that Japan and America were having problems, I was shocked. I guess I was too young to understand. I didn't believe there could be war.

"From the moment the war began, the military took over. Day after day they pounded in the idea of being good soldiers, of dedication for the glory of Japan. We even lined up to go from our dormitory to the classrooms. The food was bad. We were fed just anything that could be eaten, like sweet potato and pumpkin leaves. But no one complained. Everyone accepted this as the way life was. We didn't know anything better. We never had a taste of real freedom, so we didn't ask for freedom.

"About 1944," Paul said, "instead of going to classes, the students were put to work. I worked at the Kure Naval Base with other boys and girls. We made parts for submarines, welded, and did anything else that had to be done. Every midnight the American B-29s came. At first we used to run to the bomb shelters, but after a few months of that, we got so tired. We just tried to ignore the raids. That attitude almost cost me my life one night when bombs burned 80 percent of the city. Fires even went through the bomb shelter tunnels. To keep from suffocating in the crowded tunnels, we put our faces into the loose dirt that we scooped out of the tunnels. Many people died; many of my classmates."

He said that by the end of 1944 "we knew something was wrong. We used to wonder among ourselves—the students, not the others. We used to wonder why we were now spending all of our time digging tunnels, instead of building submarines. We used to wonder, too, why all the ships were in the harbor, instead of out in the ocean fighting. We knew it was only a matter of time before the end."

Paul was in Tokyo taking examinations to go to Waseda University when he heard that "an unusual bomb was dropped in Hiroshima City on August 6 and in Nagasaki on August 8. I was told to listen for an important message over the radio on August 15. When I heard the emperor announce the surrender, I was shocked. I felt lost. I didn't know what to do. For two days I sat at the train station to get tickets to go home to Atatashima.

"When I got to Hiroshima City, there was no station master to collect the tickets. There was no station. There was nothing but destruction. I walked around the city in a daze. I could see one end of the city to the other. There was nothing to block my line of vision. Somehow, I found someone to take me on his boat to Atatashima. I stayed home for a year. I did nothing. I had lost hope. Here I had been told to fight, fight, fight. Suddenly, everything stopped. Japan surrendered. Here I was 18 and I felt like an old, defeated man.

"Then," Paul said, his eyes sparkling, "my big brother, Ralph, came to Atatashima. What a shock. We thought he was dead. He was the first American soldier I ever saw. I recognized him right away. He was carrying a bag over his shoulder. I was so happy. I was jumping all around. I remember he walked right into the house. He didn't take his boots off. Right on the *tatami* [mat flooring] with his boots on.

"My parents were happy, too, but I think they were embarrassed at the same time. The war was still so fresh. And we had some neighbors over at the house. I remember there was talk in the village about wanting to kill Ralph, the enemy American. The people were afraid. You couldn't really blame them. They had been told over and over that the Americans were cruel ogres. They were told to keep the women in the house because the Americans would rape them. They were told to hide all valuables.

"Ralph helped to remove that fear. He didn't wear any guns or weapons when he came. He was an officer, but he looked more like a country soldier. I remember wondering why he carried his own bag. In Japan an officer doesn't carry his own bag. He would have two or three soldiers to help him. I was really proud of Ralph. I went all around and told my friends my big brother was home and had brought me this and that. The others envied me. They all wanted to see Ralph because they wanted to see what an American looked like if he weren't an ogre.

"I wore the U.S. Army hat, the U.S. Army jacket, and U.S. Army boots that Ralph gave me. I still remember the chocolate candy and gum he brought. I gobbled them up. When my mother gave me ten bars of chocolate, I would eat the ten all at once. The first time I had the candy, I remembered the taste from long ago when I was a kid in Hawaii. That taste, the smell of the downtown fish market, and my kindergarten schoolroom in Kahuku were the only things I could still remember about Hawaii."

Paul said that Ralph got really sick with malaria for a few nights. "He shook with the chills. He said he got infected in Burma. My mother scolded him because he hadn't awakened her. I remember he told my mother that nobody could help him when he got sick like that. He said he knew how to handle it by himself."

Paul recalled how excited he was to see a sleeping bag for the first time. "My mother was getting the *futon* out. Ralph said it was okay; he didn't need the *futon*. He unrolled his sleeping bag. I thought it was great."

He said that when Ralph came to visit the second time "the feeling in the village was different. He was really welcomed this time. The people were beginning to hear so many good things about the Americans. A lot of people already felt that the American rule was so much better than the Japanese military rule. I could feel people relax. Not all that tension like before."

When Ralph told them he was married and that he would be going back home to his family in Hawaii, Paul remembers being puzzled. "I couldn't understand why he didn't stay with his parents."

Other brothers started to come home from the Japanese army. Paul said, "My mother and father looked different. They looked happy that everyone had survived the war. My mother kept saying, *'Yokatta, yokatta'* [Things worked out fine]."

Paul went to Waseda University in 1946, majoring in industrial management. When he graduated, Ralph invited him to come to Hawaii. "I was happy. Man, it was like going to the land of my dreams," Paul said. "But when I got to Honolulu in 1951, at age 24, I had to start from the beginning to learn to speak and to write English. It was tough and I started to lose confidence in myself. I wanted to go back to Japan so badly, but I decided to stick with it because if I left then, I would never have another chance."

Paul's father died in 1952. Paul said, "I felt bad I wasn't there with him. My father was very strict and short-tempered. I remember once when I was 7 or 8, I took his pillow from under his head. He got really angry. I hid all night until my aunt came to rescue me. But after my father got older, he began to mellow. During the winter nights, I remember he used to come in and cover me up, instead of my mother. I admired him. He hardly went to school, but he was very learned."

It was in 1952 that the U.S. Army notified Paul to get a physical because he was a dual citizen. He said, "The X-rays showed spots in my chest. I had tuberculosis." He was at Leahi Hospital for a year and a half. While there he took regular high school classes and a special English course. "I used to read the *Star-Bulletin* thoroughly. I'd mark down all the words I didn't know and then look them up in the dictionary."

After he was released, he had all kinds of jobs—radio and TV announcer, Japanese language teacher, carpenter, liquor salesman, and bakery manager. At the time of the interview in 1966, he was the advertising manager for the *Hawaii hochi* (a bilingual newspaper) where he worked for ten years.

His wife (Florence Honda) was also born in Hawaii and raised in Japan. Paul said, "I always talked about going back to Japan, but when I went there in 1965, I knew I really belonged in Hawaii. This is my home. I was actually afraid when I got to Japan. So many changes. I didn't feel that I had come home. I felt lost. And, you know," he added, "I had always thought Atatashima was my home. I found out it wasn't anymore. That's now the home of my brother Goro's children. Not mine. When I returned to the Honolulu airport, I knew I had come home. I knew, too, that I wanted my three children to be raised as Americans."

Donald Yempuku was surprised, in 1966, to find that he still felt so emotional when talking about an incident that happened twenty-one years before. "It was just before the surrender ceremony in Hong Kong on September 16, 1945. I was the interpreter for the Japanese military officials. As we came down the stairs in single file, there was a big crowd in the lobby of the Peninsula Hotel. We—the defeated—were a source of curiosity.

Paul Yempuku, 1966.
*Star-Bulletin Photo.*

Everyone was staring at us. About midway down the staircase, I saw his back. I saw my oldest brother Ralph's back. He was in an American uniform. I knew it was Ralph right away. Immediately, I was happy he was alive. But almost in the same breath, I was embarrassed because he was on the side of the enemy.

"For a brief second, I felt the urge to call out. But I couldn't let myself do that. I just couldn't do it. In my mind the war was still going on and we were still enemies. It was the most trying moment of my life as I marched past Ralph and past the crowd. I was so glad Ralph was distracted at that moment and didn't see me. I knew the only way I could make it was to keep my eyes straight ahead. I glued my eyes to the officer in front of me."

Donald shook his head and stared at his hands as he told the story. He said, "After the ceremony, I sent word home to my parents that Ralph was alive. There had been no word from Ralph all through the war. We all thought he had died."

He saw Ralph again in February 1946, in Kyoto. "This time," he said, "we shook hands. Japanese, you know, never show much emotion. We didn't discuss the war. I felt that we were all fortunate to have come out alive. Ralph felt that way, too." Donald said, "I still feel the war shouldn't have happened. I'll say this. I'm glad the Japanese military lost. War never settles anything. All it does is to create more problems."

He recalled the night before the war started. "I was 24 and working the evening shift at the *Domei News Service*. I knew something was in the air. All the important people were around. Then the word of the attack came in. We had an extra edition out at 6 or 7 A.M. The headline said something about Japanese forces enter state of war with the United States in the western Pacific. The bombing of Pearl Harbor was secondary because attacks had taken place at the same time in Manila and Malaya.

"I felt bad that it was the United States, because a part of me was American. It was a real tragedy. The two countries that were part of me. I knew I had to choose. I did a lot of soul-searching. When I came to Japan with my family, I had just graduated from McKinley High School. I went to Japanese school in Hiroshima and then to college there. In school, patriotism was really drummed into us. I remember at first I didn't know what was going on when I saw everyone bowing low in front of the emperor's picture. I got a good scolding for not bowing.

"I went back to Hawaii briefly in March of 1941 after graduation. While I was going to school in Japan, I had wanted to go back to Hawaii so badly. But when I did go, I couldn't get a good job. No way to get ahead. I didn't feel right. I preferred being back in Japan. I hadn't realized that it would be like that. I felt torn—half and half. But, Japan pulled me more. So I came back to Japan.

"In view of all that background, I made my choice when the war came. I threw my support behind Japan. I told myself, 'I'm Japanese now. I can't be loyal to two countries.' But I still didn't want to fight America."

He worked for the *Domei News Service* and the military

press bureau as a translator in Tokyo and in Hong Kong. "Because I was still a U.S. citizen, military police visited my parents two or three times to investigate. You see, Atatashima, where my parents lived and where my mother is still living, is in a strategic location. From the island you can see all the ship movements around there.

"I filed for Japanese citizenship and lost my U.S. citizenship. I regretted that I couldn't be a citizen of both countries. But I'm content with my choice now and have no regrets. My roots are here. My wife and my children. This is my home. I'm 50 now. Only eighteen of those years were spent in Hawaii. The rest in Japan. This is my home now. This is where I want to die."

Donald said, "I hope, though, that my three children will be able to visit the United States some day. I want them to go there and understand the United States. I want them to know the country where I was born."

Ralph, the oldest of the five brothers, was the only one in the family who didn't leave for Japan in 1933. In an interview in Honolulu in 1966, Ralph described December 7, 1941 as "one of the strangest days in my life. I was 27 and was working as an assistant graduate manager for the University of Hawaii's athletic department. A couple of mainland football teams were staying at the Moana Hotel, and we were going to take them sightseeing. The tour was cancelled when we learned of the attack.

"I was driving back when I saw some naval flyers in Waikiki frantically looking for a ride back to their carrier in Pearl Harbor. There were no cabs and no streetcars around. I gave them a ride. I remember stopping to get Bromo Seltzer for them because they had been on quite a drinking spree. Before reaching the Pearl Harbor gate, I saw all those dead bodies piled like sardines in a truck. The sight scared the hell out of me.

"It's sort of naive, I guess, but I never thought that war would come. I had been a freshman at the university when my family left for Japan. I had to work hard to support myself and didn't have much time to sit down and think about what was going on in the world. For days after the attack, I kept asking myself: 'Why the hell did the Japanese want to do something like that?' I never once thought of myself as anything other than an American, but my family was there in Japan. I looked Japanese. My name is Japanese.

"I remember when I talked with people of other racial backgrounds, I felt uncomfortable for a while. Like Japan's attack was kind of my fault. I kept thinking: 'Why did Japan do it? It's so embarrassing. It's so uncomfortable for me.' I'm sure others felt the same way, including German Americans and Italian Americans. Whenever I filled out questionnaires that asked where my family was, I felt kind of bad—not really guilty, but sensitive. I knew my brothers would have to be in the Japanese army because they were of age.

"I had the feeling that because my family was there, I—even more than other nisei—must prove my loyalty to America. Right after Pearl Harbor the Hawaii Territorial Guard was organized. I had an ROTC officer's commission. Quite a few American Japanese, mostly university students, joined the guard. We stayed with it for about three months.

"There was a lot of criticism about 'the Japs' being allowed to carry rifles and guarding areas like the harbor. Some people were saying: 'The Japs are taking over.' So, early in 1942, the guard was disbanded—only long enough to get the nisei out— and then it was reorganized without 'the Japs'. We nisei couldn't do anything about it. But we didn't want to just sit back and do nothing. We wanted to do something. About 150 of us, mainly university kids, formed the Varsity Victory Volunteers. Primarily, we were used as a labor battalion for the engineers. We didn't care how menial the work was as long as we could help. We did road construction, dug ditches, and strung barbed wire. Because I was older than the other boys, I was asked to supervise the group.

"I should point out that there was a lot of hot and serious racial opposition in the community against us. So we didn't

Lieutenant General Delos C. Emmons, commanding general of the Hawaiian War Department, commending Ralph Yempuku for his lead in organizing the nisei Varsity Victory Volunteers, 1942. *Yempuku Photo Collection.*

know whether we'd get kicked in the pants again for being 'Japs'.

"A great deal of credit goes to the members of the Hawaii Emergency Service Committee who worked with the community and counseled us. People like the late Charles R. Hemenway, Hung Wai Ching, Masaji Marumoto, Baron Goto, Katsuro Miho, Dr. Ernest Murai, and others. Jack Burns, too.

"Hemenway was a really great person. He was a big, big shot with Hawaiian Trust. He was chairman of the board. He was also chairman of the university's Board of Regents. He was one of the few big shots who really understood how we felt. He sincerely felt that the nisei could be trusted as much as any other American and stood up for us. Many, many haoles and other ethnic groups just didn't trust us. Of course, I didn't blame them, really, because Japan was at war with the United States. It was just a case of us having to show them that we could be trusted; that we were Americans, too.

"It wasn't until March of 1943 that Washington gave the okay for the nisei to join the U.S. Army. The 442nd Regimental Combat Team was formed and a whole mob of Hawaii nisei boys volunteered.

"I couldn't get in because of a bad knee. But I wanted to get in really badly. I talked with some officials. They said they'd accept me if I could pass a ranger training course. For two weeks, I went through the paces of ranger training—and then, the final physical exam. I passed. I joined the other nisei boys already at Camp Shelby in Mississippi and then moved to Fort Benning, Georgia, for officer training.

"One day, an official from Washington came down to ask if any of the nisei boys would volunteer for the Office of Strategic Services. We had heard about the good work the cloak-and-dagger outfit was doing in Europe, so I volunteered, along with three other Hawaii nisei officers—Chiyoki Ikeda, Junichi Buto, and Dick Betsui.

"We were sent to Camp Savage for a concentrated course in Japanese, radio training, and ranger training. It was then that we found out that we were going to fight the Japanese, not the Germans.

"Our all-nisei OSS team consisted of four officers and a dozen enlisted men. We went to Burma by way of Europe and India. While the OSS is considered an intelligence outfit, our job was mostly combat work with guerrilla forces. We would parachute in behind enemy lines and organize guerrilla troops and supply them with arms and ammunition for ambush operations.

"I worked in Myitkyina, Bhamo, and Lashio and helped organize the Kachins, war tribes of North Burma who were mercenaries. In Burma, I used to be scared. I used to think: 'What if I'm confronted by my brothers? What would I do?' These thoughts would come to mind as we prepared for ambush at night: 'Jesus! What would happen if one of my brothers is in that convoy? What if my brother is among the prisoners I have to interrogate?'

"I knew, of course, that whatever happened, I could never jeopardize our troops. I told myself that if one of my brothers should be caught in an ambush, he would be caught in an ambush—that's all. You know, so much of war is placing personal feelings aside.

"When the Japanese were finally chased out of Burma, we moved up the Burma Road to Kunming in West China. We were to operate the same way we did in Burma—but the war ended. And that's when I heard about the destruction of Hiroshima. I wondered whether my parents had died. And what about my brothers? Were they dead too, or were they prisoners?

"I knew my parents lived on Atatashima near Hiroshima City, but I had no idea just how near Hiroshima it was. I didn't have time to make any inquiries because we were rushed out to mercy missions. The Americans were afraid the Japanese would execute American prisoners of war. Our job was to parachute into Japanese bases and liberate American and Allied prisoners.

"I led one jump into a POW camp on Hainan Island on the southern coast of China. We freed two- or three-hundred prisoners. They were Australian and Dutch imprisoned since 1939–1940, but no Americans. The Australians were in good shape because they had leadership and discipline and they took care of each other. The Dutch didn't, so we found out they were dying at a rate of two a day from infections and malnutrition.

"About a month later, I went to Hong Kong on a British cruiser to witness the surrender ceremonies at the Peninsula Hotel. It was there that my brother, Donald, saw me. I wasn't aware that he was there and went on back to Kunming. A short while later, a Honolulu friend came to my tent and told me he had seen my brother, Donald, in a POW camp in Hong Kong. He said: 'I saw this guy who looked exactly like you. I thought for a moment that you were on OSS duty there. But after observing this guy for a while I knew it wasn't you.'

"My friend said he got curious and asked the POW if he had a brother in Hawaii. That's when Donald told my friend that he had seen me at the Hong Kong surrender. Wow! I didn't know what I should do—should I go and see my brother or not? I wondered what Donald would do if he were in my place. Before I could decide, I was sent to Shanghai because I was eligible to return home for discharge. But instead of going home I wanted to go to Japan first to look for my parents. So I volunteered for the U.S. Counter Intelligence Corps in Tokyo and Kyoto.

"First chance I got, I headed for Hiroshima. I didn't know the country. All I knew was that my parents lived on a tiny island called Atatashima near Hiroshima City. The train official had never heard of the place. When I got to Hiroshima City, I was shocked—there was nothing there but devastation. The whole city was wiped out. I thought my parents really must be dead. I left Hiroshima City thinking that.

"But later, I decided to try again. This time, I went further into Hiroshima. I asked people along the way and finally found a man who said he could take me out to Atatashima in his skiff.

"Night had fallen when I got to Atatashima. When my mother answered my knock, she didn't know who I was until I said 'Okasan [mother].' My father almost had another stroke.

They were convinced that I had died because of all the weird propaganda that they had been hearing about the slaughter of nisei.

"I brought food rations and other goods like soap for the people on the island in later visits because I knew my parents would be under suspicion with me—an enemy captain—visiting them. A lot of those families had lost sons, brothers, and fathers in the war. Later, I got together with my brothers. We were happy to see each other. There was none of the 'Gee, you were the enemy' kind of thing. Nothing like that."

Finally, in 1946, Ralph returned to Honolulu. The idea of being back seemed unreal. He said, "I kept thinking that I would get up in the middle of this dream and find myself back in Burma." But he didn't. It was real—even his prewar clothes that his wife, the former Gladys Ito, had neatly packed away for him.

Since his return, Ralph has been in the promotion and management end of show business, starting with the Lau Yee Chai nightclub. He then went into business for himself as a show and sports promoter. He recently retired as a colonel in the Army Reserve.

Looking back at the war, Ralph said: "The war was a blessing in disguise for American nisei. If it wasn't for the war and the nisei's part in that war, we would never have had Spark Matsunaga, Dan Inouye, or Patsy Takemoto Mink serving in Congress. We would never have had all those nisei in high government positions and professions today. Many Islanders felt they were treated as second class citizens before Hawaii got statehood. The Japanese in Hawaii before the war were third class citizens. They dropped to tenth class when Japan bombed Pearl Harbor.

"When the nisei took the bull by the horns and fought to prove themselves, a lot of them got killed. But they didn't die in vain. They enabled the nisei to advance politically, socially, and economically. The change for the nisei has been dramatic.

Today, my two sons and other AJA kids don't face any of that business of not feeling 100 percent trusted as the nisei felt before, especially in the early part of the war. This is why I feel the nisei boys who died didn't die in vain. They made a helluva lot possible for coming generations."

---

■

## 1990 Update

The five Yempuku brothers had their first reunion in Hawaii in fifty-three years in June of 1986 when they assembled for the wedding of Paul's son Wayne.

"It was fun," said Paul. While Goro, Toru, and Donald had visited before, "this was different," he said. "We were all together. We went to Kahuku, where we grew up. Our old house was gone, but so many memories—that pine tree that so and so planted, that house where so and so used to live, and all kinds of stories about the old days."

Paul is grateful the reunion was held then because two years later Donald, now 73, suffered a stroke, which left him semi-paralyzed. He had been in the import-export business. He is in a care home in Mito City, fairly close to Tokyo, where his wife and two of their three children reside.

Their mother, Mrs. Gofuyo Yempuku, outlived her husband by twenty-six years. She died in Atatashima in 1978 at age 88.

Ralph, the eldest Yempuku, is now 75. Despite heart bypass surgery several years ago, he is still on a full schedule as a promoter of shows and sports events, mostly in Japan. His office and home are, however, in Honolulu. He and his wife, Gladys, have two sons.

Toru, 71, who worked for many years as a translator for the American government in Tokyo, is now retired and lives with his wife in Zushi City. They have two sons.

The Yempuku brothers in a 1986 Hawaii reunion portrait. Front, *left* to *right,* Ralph and Donald. Back, Paul, Toru, and Goro. *Yempuku Photo Collection.*

Goro, 69, will soon pass on his duties as the Buddhist priest for the village of Atatashima to his son, Nobuyuki, now his assistant. His son is also running the school on the island.

Paul, 63, was named publisher of the *Hawaii hochi,* the only Japanese bilingual daily newspaper in Hawaii, in 1967 at age 39. He and his wife, Florence, live in Honolulu. They have three children.

Asked to sum up the family's war years, Paul said, "We were really lucky. We all came through okay."

# Chapter 5

##  THE MIYASATO STORY

I t was one of those lovely November days in California in 1966. Albert Hajime Miyasato, 41, agreed to put aside his work on his dissertation at the University of Southern California in Los Angeles for an interview that he knew would be emotionally taxing and, therefore, dreaded. He said his insides still churned whenever someone would ask him: "And what did you do during the war, Al?"

Miyasato sighed. "That kind of thing still shakes me up. Intellectually, I tell myself I need not feel that way. But at the gut level, I still do. I still feel squeamish. Awkward. Uncomfortable."

He paused and his voice dropped. "I was a traitor. I was willing to die for Japan. I was willing to die for the emperor. I gloried in what the military leadership called 'the cause of the Greater East Asia Co-Prosperity Sphere'. The leaders called it a new world order in Asia. It was Japan's grand expansionist plan. I was completely brainwashed. I would have volunteered for the *Kamikaze* Youth Corps had I had my Japanese citizenship.

"That's why I say, I was a traitor. That's why I still feel so uncomfortable when people start talking about the war. Inevitably, someone will ask: 'Were you in the army, Al?' Sometimes I volunteer the information before I'm asked, or I say that it's a long story—I was on the wrong side. I've learned to control my reaction in such situations much better now by anticipating and gaining control in that way.

97

"I used to be really uncomfortable when I first got back from Japan, especially with my nisei friends who had served so honorably and courageously with the 442nd Regimental Combat Team or in the Pacific. Here, those nisei men had fought so bravely for the United States and I, meanwhile, had been on the wrong side. This feeling still hangs on today. It is constantly there."

Miyasato's war within himself dates back to a summer's day in 1940 when he was 14 and just graduated from Washington Intermediate School. On that day he left Honolulu with his mother, Mrs. Shohei Miyasato, aboard the *Asama maru*, supposedly on a summer trip. "But," he said, "my parents had a secret motive.

"After traveling throughout Japan, I was asked to stay there to study and to live in a temple in Yawata City, Fukuoka, as an acolyte for later ministerial training. My mother and father wanted that, so I agreed. My mother returned to Hawaii and I remained at the Keikoji Temple in Yawata. My mentor was the Bishop Horyu Onuma, one of the best Jodo Shinshu Buddhist priests in the country."

It was while Miyasato attended Yawata Middle School that the war began. He remembers the day: "We students were assembled in the field. Talk of war circulated . . . a gloomy day . . . people clustered around radios . . . people clapped their hands and yelled 'Banzai!' as reports tallied the number of American planes destroyed and American ships sunk."

In Hawaii Miyasato's parents were deeply distressed when they heard the news about Pearl Harbor. Mr. Miyasato said, "I knew my son wouldn't be in the military service because of his age and because he was an American citizen, not a Japanese citizen. I had never registered him for dual citizenship because I always felt a person should be a citizen of one country at a time. My wife and I figured our son would be placed in a labor battalion. We bled inside as we thought of all the suffering he would have to go through."

In his Japanese schoolroom young Miyasato observed with

Albert Miyasato dressed
for a formal portrait while
a student at a Buddhist
temple in wartime Japan.
*Miyasato Photo Collection.*

amazement how rapidly school life was being taken over by the
military. He said, "There were all the overtones of military
dominance. After a few months, I was thoroughly brainwashed. Although I wistfully thought of my parents and
younger brothers and sisters in Hawaii, I found myself willing
to die for the emperor at any time. Like all my classmates, I was
caught up in the cause of the Greater East Asia Co-Prosperity
Sphere.

"As the war grew more intense, many of my classmates left
school to volunteer for the *Kamikaze* [Divine Wind] Youth
Corps. The class got smaller and smaller. Within a year-and-a-
half, one-third of the students had gone. And some of them had
already died in that time. I would have gone with them, but I
wasn't a Japanese citizen."

Because he was an alien, Miyasato was forced out of the
Yawata area, where the biggest steel mill in the Far East was

located. It was an official fortified zone. So, early in 1943, he was sent to Tokyo in the custody of the Japanese Foreign Office, which operated a special school called Heishikan for nisei such as Miyasato. It was started some four years before the war. A lineup of courses was taught, including English, shorthand, political economics, and one on morals and ethics called *shushin*. The morals and ethics class studied the character of men like Admiral Togo and Japan's feudal lords. Occasional mention was made of contemporary Japanese military figures. Miyasato said an equivalent class in the United States would have focused on men like Abraham Lincoln.

Miyasato said, "The Foreign Office gave us free room and board, plus 50 yen as spending money for books, movies, and live shows. There were a lot of films, shows, and sumo wrestling for morale. In return, we were to work for Radio Tokyo or the *Nippon Times* after we completed school. I only had some practice sessions in announcing. We never really got to work.

"The Heishikan was classified as a spy school by the U.S. State Department immediately after the war. It really was no such thing. Because of the daily air raids, we just subsisted on a day-to-day basis. We were, if anything, taking advantage of the Japanese government by living at their expense. But this association almost cost me my U.S. citizenship after the war."

As the war continued, "life became more and more harsh," he said. "Daily and nightly, the B-29s came. Twice we were hit directly. Fortunately, we were able to put out the fires that threatened to gut the ancient building we lived in. The Japanese were so well organized to cope with such disasters."

He lived with about thirty nisei, including two from Hawaii. Most of them spoke English fluently and Japanese only haltingly. The majority returned to the United States after the war.

Miyasato said, "The metro and military police watched us constantly. Most of the Japanese stayed away from us. We were restricted to an area of about fifty miles in radius and had to get special permission from the police to leave the confines. Food and clothing were almost impossible to buy. At times, we went to the Chiba countryside with our clothing to bargain illegally with farmers for food. When we got caught, the police were rough on us. A number of the boys got beaten up.

"But we were hungry all the time. Always—hungry, hungry, hungry. Here I was, supposed to be at my sexual peak, and I never thought about sex, only about food, during all my waking hours. I used to crave good rice and sugar and Chinese cracked seeds. Our diet consisted of a daily handful of junk rice —rice mixed with soybeans—which looked like bagasse [residue from sugar cane processing] because all the oil had been extracted from them. With that we ate dried fish or old vegetables. No sugar, no coffee, no tea. No one trusted the cook. We suspected her of hoarding and playing favorites. Each person thought the other was getting more food than he was."

Not surprisingly, Miyasato's feelings toward Japan began to change after he was forced to stay in Tokyo. He said, "When I had first come to Japan, I felt I was Japanese. I looked like everyone else. I was treated like everyone else. Now, they treated me differently. I was no longer like everyone else. I was different. And I was being persecuted for being different. I almost had a nervous breakdown. We weren't mistreated physically, for the most part. The mistreatment was subtle—through the police. We were followed, questioned if we had an English book, and harassed.

"Things got really bad in Tokyo in 1945 because of the continuous air raids. There was talk of an American invasion of Japan. A Mr. Sukeyuki Akamatsu, who was in charge of us for the Foreign Office, evacuated our group to his rest home on the slopes of Mt. Fuji. I understand Mr. Akamatsu served briefly with the consulate in Hawaii around 1925. He took a lot of abuse from others for helping us. Just before the war ended, I was taken back to Yawata.

"It was a tremendous relief when the war ended. I didn't care who won as long as it was over and I could see my family again. I had not heard from them all through the long war. I've thought about that often—the fact that I had had no feelings whatsoever about who won the war. I was only concerned about my personal relief."

The Miyasatos in Hawaii felt the same way. "We just rejoiced that the war was over. We were happy because the end meant that we would be seeing our son."

Mr. Miyasato, a travel agent, helped to maintain the Jikoen Temple in Kalihi during the war. He said, "All the Buddhist temples were closed down. Most of the priests had been taken to internment camps. And the people were afraid to go to the temples for fear they would be taken too." He said he prayed constantly for the end of the war and his son's safe return.

Albert Miyasato said that in Yawata, "I literally heard the war end as all the noisy machinery in the steel mills ground to a sudden halt. Silence—what was that! Everything just stopped. As the emperor announced the surrender on the radio, men, women, and children cried. I guess they were crying for different reasons. But, they cried."

After the war Miyasato served as an interpreter for the Japanese military police in their surrender of arms to the American forces. American officers from the 11th Airborne Division took Miyasato and the other nisei with him in Yawata to be their interpreter-translators. "I was so happy to work with the United States. I detested the Japanese for all the harassment and stress," he said.

Then, Miyasato got a letter from the American Consul that he had no American protection in Japan because of his association with what the United States called the "spy school" (Heishikan). Miyasato said, "That meant that I had no rights as an American while I was there. And, of course, I had no protection from the Japanese government because I was not a Japanese citizen. In order to get my passport back and return to Hawaii, I had to establish my whereabouts in Japan with affidavits verifying my every move during the war. That took me eighteen months."

It was during that period that Miyasato had written to his family: "If I do get my papers, I will be a happy man. That will be the greatest moment in my whole life, which I shall always cherish. It really is a slow process, but if a man has enough patience, it will get him where he wants to go." He finally gòt his passport on April 1, 1947, and returned to Honolulu aboard a converted Liberty ship. He had been away for six years and nine months. Through the blur of tears, he spotted his family right away. His family, too, saw him quickly. They wept as they observed how thin he was; how much taller he was; how his face hadn't really changed at all.

Miyasato said: "It sounds mushy, but for a brief moment, I did not recognize the fragrance of fresh flower leis. But, quickly, I remembered the wonderful smells. That really brought me back."

His father said, "We felt so sorry for him. What should have been his happy, carefree years had turned out to be years of sorrow and suffering."

Albert Miyasato's homecoming as recorded in this *Hawaii Times* photo showing his mother, Mrs. Shohei Miyasato, reaching for him across a dockside barrier. *Star-Bulletin Photo.*

Miyasato remembers speaking to a Japanese community group shortly after his return on the question of whether Japan had lost or won the war. There was still a group of Japanese at that time who refused to believe that Japan had lost. "After I told them about the devastation and the defeat," he said, "a few of them came up and bawled me out for saying that the United States had won. They accused me of being a tool for the American government. It was to help clear up the confusion that the Club 100 veterans put on a play, *The Defeated*, in 1948. I wanted to help, so I acted in it."

He entered the University of Hawaii Teachers' College and found the adjustment almost overwhelming at times. "For example," he said, "it was not easy to participate in free discussion. All my training in Japan was geared to subservience in thinking. It was a difficult burden to think for myself again after years of being controlled in thought and in action. I just didn't know how to think for myself. I felt the democratic process placed a severe burden on the individual. I forced myself to participate in student activities at the expense of studies. I'm glad I didn't give up."

In 1966, at age 41, Miyasato received his doctorate in education from the University of Southern California under a fellowship from a U.S.C. support group and from the Hawaii Community Foundation Scholarship Fund. Prior to working on his doctorate he had served the Hawaii Department of Education as a staff specialist in personnel for the Hawaii district.

Miyasato is married to the former Shizue Kuwahara of Hilo, a longtime schoolteacher.

Miyasato reflected: "Somehow, despite all the hardships brought on by war, I've always felt that this dark chapter in my life helped me to become a better teacher. It's the kind of thing that you can't get by reading. The more I look back on that difficult interlude in Japan, I can't help marveling at the power of education. How a whole nation could be swayed into thinking and acting in a certain way by a systematic, organized method of education continues to astound me. I guess that's why I feel so strongly committed to my profession."

Shohei Miyasato in 1966.
*Star-Bulletin Photo.*

## 1990 Update

The first thing Albert Miyasato said in an update interview was: "I want you to know how much that story about my wartime experiences helped me. It was very therapeutic. It brought my feelings right out there instead of being bottled up."

Miyasato, 65, is retired as an educator. He is now active as a fifth-term president of the Honpa Hongwanji Mission in Honolulu. He also holds a part-time job with the U.S. Pacific Joint Command Headquarters briefing visiting Japanese officials about the military organization.

He was a consultant in Saudi Arabia from 1981 to 1984 for the development of a city school system in Yanbu. Before that he was a deputy superintendent and a district superintendent for Hawaii's public schools. He was also an administrative assistant to former Governor George Ariyoshi.

Miyasato has been a frequent visitor to Japan since the war—after he got over the emotional block about ever going back there. "I resisted it for years," he said, "nothing but bad memories."

Then, in 1974, he was called to take a work-related trip to Japan. "I was just amazed at the number of people in Japan today. What's more, everyone looked like me. That was surprising to me because as a kid during the war, I had felt so different —I wasn't one of them and I was always tense about that."

"As I grow older," Miyasato said, "I have good feelings for both countries—the United States and Japan. When I came back to Hawaii after the war, I had this tremendous sense of gratitude and commitment to the United States. Now I can look back and appreciate the good things I learned in Japan, too, like respect for your elders, self-discipline, and kindness that quite a few people showed me during those days."

Miyasato and his wife, Shizue, live in Honolulu. They have three daughters. His father, Shohei Miyasato, died in 1970 at age 70. His mother died in 1982 at age 82.

# Chapter 6

---
•
---

# THE FUJIWARA STORY

**R**obert Teruto Fujiwara grew up in the sugar plantation town of Honokaa on the island of Hawaii. In 1938, when he was 14 and his sister 10, they left for Japan with their parents. His father, stricken with cancer, wanted to return to his birthplace. Because Robert was a dual citizen, he was drafted into the Japanese army during the war. On August 6, 1945, at 21, Robert was stationed in Hiroshima City. The following is his story as told in an interview in Tokyo in 1966.

"It was after breakfast. I was on the second floor of our wooden barracks building. A few other Japanese soldiers were in the long room, too. I walked across the room. I had my shirt off. I guess I was scratching my back when I heard the sound of a plane. I poked my head out of the window. 'It's going to be another hot day,' I thought, as I looked around for the plane. I couldn't spot it, so I started to withdraw from the window.

"In that fraction of a second, I saw it. I saw the bright yellow flash. Not like lightning. More blinding. I remember yelling my head off. I knew I was burned. I ran to the door. The building began to shake. The next thing I knew, I was on the ground. In the middle of ruins. The barracks had collapsed.

"My head hurt. There was a lump. I climbed out. I was bleeding. My arms. My chest. My stomach. My skin was dark purple. I touched my arm. The skin came right off—easily. I knew something was really wrong. I went toward the dispensary. It was in ruins. Everyone was yelling. All that yelling.

"One of the officers told us to evacuate to the mountains

nearby. We ran. Thirty minutes . . . 500 yards. My burns ached. Raw. The burns . . . one-third of my body. My arms. My chest. My stomach. Just a little on my face. I guess the eaves of the building protected my face.

"I stayed up in the mountains for hours. It was getting dark. I went down. A medical officer examined me. He put oil all over. So much pain, I didn't feel anything. I lay out in the open—bare —that night. I could hear the groans. But it was real quiet.

"The next day came. I walked a few miles to a village. A temporary hospital. I stayed there one night. The next day, I was on a train. Three hours in the mountains. Another temporary place. A school. I stayed there for two months. That's when I suffered. The burns. Death would have been too kind. I can't put it into words. I couldn't move my arms. I was flat on my back. Just lying there . . . I couldn't move.

"Newspapers on my body . . . pus . . . the newspapers wouldn't come off. They took me to the serious section. One to a mat. Sixty mats. Side by side. We were guinea pigs. They didn't know what to use. They tried layers of oil. White. Pink. Yellow. And blood transfusions. I didn't eat anything, except boiled rice broth. I don't remember fever.

"My mother came. It was amazing she found me. She was living in Iwakuni. She said she almost went to Hiroshima City that day. I was glad she didn't. And I was glad my sister Tokie was okay.

"You know, I knew I would recover. I had faith in myself. After two months, I could get up. Gradually, I could get around. I could go home now.

"A flood had ripped the railroad tracks. I walked a whole day and stayed overnight in a farm house. I got a ride the next day on a truck to the train. One station before home, the rails were washed out. I walked again. A few hours and I made it. Home.

"My weight was down to nothing. Before I was burned, I weighed about 60 kilos [132 pounds]. I was down to 45 kilos [99 pounds].

"I recuperated at home for three months before looking for

work. I had a lot of time to think. All that time I was flat on my back. All that time I was at home. Many thoughts. Every so often, I would be surprised that I was still living. Bitter against the United States? I would be lying if I said I didn't feel bitter.

"Even today, the word leukemia haunts me. Every time I feel sick, that word . . . it haunts me. The scars. They're a part of me. Every day. I see the scars . . . reminds me . . . I'm okay now. But I'm always on guard. My blood count is low, but not dangerous. I guess I worry too much.

"Things like this nobody can understand. You must be a victim to understand. The terror . . . the worries . . . I try not to, but . . . Today, I think, it's all just fate. Destiny. At first, I couldn't figure what the bomb was. I knew it was something big. Something pretty big. I used to think a lot about Hawaii all that time. I still think a lot about Hawaii. That's my dream. To go for a vacation. See my friends. You know, Honokaa. I wonder if they're still there. Yes, I think about Hawaii.

"During the war, I was so confused. I liked the two countries. Deep down, I was an American. And yet, I felt I had to do my duty when the Japanese army called. I was so confused. Even now, deep inside, I feel I'm Hawaiian. And yet, I'm Japanized. It's kind of funny how things happen.

"As a kid, I was a real Honokaa boy. My father and mother [Mr. and Mrs. Shinjiro Fujiwara] ran a store and a restaurant. Homemade noodles and homemade jelly rolls and pies. We all helped out. In 1938, my father got sick. Liver cancer. My parents closed the business. My sister Tokie and I left with my parents for Japan. My two older brothers, Hiromi and Isami [Harry], stayed in Honolulu with relatives.

"My father died in Japan a year later. He was 49. My mother, we . . . well, everybody had a hard time during the war and after the war. Tokie worked at a Catholic orphanage in Hiroshima.

"I was in Japanese high school when the war started. We did a lot of labor work around army compounds. I was drafted in 1944 and was stationed in Hiroshima. At first, I thought Japan

A last snapshot of the Fujiwara family taken before leaving for Japan in 1938. Robert is at *left* and Tokie is between her parents. Hiromi, who remained in Hawaii, is at *right*. Isami (Harry), who also stayed, is not pictured. *Fujiwara Photo Collection.*

was winning the war. There was no news in the army. But, toward the end, I figured Japan must be losing. The officers wouldn't say we were losing.

"There was no word from my brothers in Hawaii all through the war. I worried about them. I figured they'd be in the army too. I guess I didn't even want to think about what would happen if we came face-to-face during the war. After the war, I heard that my brother, Hiromi, was with the 442nd Regimental Combat Team in Europe.

"It was rough in the Japanese army. Not because I was half-American. The training was rough. I didn't talk much. Just a matter of doing what they told me to do. I don't want any more war. It was a hard lesson. No sense to war.

"I tried a lot of different jobs after I got well. Now, I'm settled in newspaper work. I've been with the *Yomiuri shimbun* for ten years. I'm a proofreader for the English section. Things are expensive in Tokyo. I have to work almost two shifts—from 6 or 7 in the morning to 5 P.M.

"I got married two years ago. My wife was a victim of the bomb too. She got blown out of her house. But she didn't get burned. We want to have children, but we have fears. We have fears . . . abnormal children or something. A friend who was also a victim had a child. The child died. My wife's not too strong. I worry about her. Maybe the aftereffects . . .

"It's hard to talk about things like this. You have to be a victim to know."

Suddenly Fujiwara noticed the time and said in bewilderment: "Have I been talking all that time? I've been talking too much. I didn't know I was going to talk like that. I didn't mean to talk so much."

Even days after the interview in Tokyo, Fujiwara, 43, was disturbed about the stream of words that had flowed from within him. He telephoned numerous times, hoping to withdraw the story.

Painfully shy by nature, he found it upsetting to think that so much of himself would see print. He finally approved the publication of his story. He said, "It was a hard lesson. I wonder if people care. You have to be a victim to know. That's why I wonder about the story. I wonder if anyone would really care."

Robert's brothers in Honolulu—Hiromi, an accountant, and Harry, a carpenter—had steadfastly refused to be interviewed for the 1966 story. Their reluctance reflects the tenor of the times. They finally agreed to be interviewed in their homes in 1985, about the time that Japanese Americans began feeling comfortable about discussing the war period.

Hiromi and Harry would say little about Robert's A-bomb injuries, except that it was "fate." Harry conveyed his feelings indirectly by recalling his visit to the Hiroshima Peace Museum in 1965: "When I saw the very first photograph of an A-bomb victim, I wanted to run and yell, 'What have we done! What have we done!' I had such bad feelings inside of me. Everything in that museum made me feel 'Wow! We are the ones who dropped that bomb.' I felt really strange inside of me. That's when I started to realize what my brother [Robert] went through."

Harry spent the war years as a carpenter building military barracks. At Hickam Air Force Base on Oahu, he said, workers of Japanese descent wore black ID tags while caucasians wore white tags.

The one wartime joy, he said, was seeing major league stars like Joe DiMaggio perform in games in the old stadium. "People lined up for hours to get in. DiMaggio's plane was two hours late, but not a single person left. Good thing. He hit a home run."

Hiromi Fujiwara of the 442nd poses with Polish women liberated by his unit from a German camp near Augsburg, Germany, in 1945. *Fujiwara Photo Collection.*

But uppermost in Harry's mind all through the war, he said, was "worry about my family in Japan, because a family without the head man can run into trouble with people making fun, giving a rough time, or even taking advantage, unless the mother is strong or a strong son takes over. I don't know why people are like that but they are."

Hiromi was worried, too, as he battled through Italy, France, and Germany with the 442nd. "I will never forget the smell of dead people all around me . . . the miserable cold of that winter campaign in the Vosges Mountains to rescue the 'Texas Lost Battalion' . . . the scene of thousands of Jews in their striped uniforms walking aimlessly through the German countryside. I'll never forget that scene as long as I live."

---

# 1990 Update

Robert Fujiwara, 66, retired several years ago as a partner in a small publishing venture in Tokyo. To celebrate, he vacationed in Hawaii—his dream ever since he left his boyhood life in Honokaa on the island of Hawaii in 1938.

His Honolulu brothers—Harry, 72, and Hiromi, 68—said Robert was so happy being back that he and his wife returned a year later. They visited Honokaa and "feasted" on hotdogs, Spam, Vienna sausage, and other favorites that he hadn't had for nearly fifty years. That reminded Hiromi that when his mother was urged to make a list for a CARE package after the war, her requests included red coconut ball candy, canned pork and beans, *"ka-li"* (curry powder), ingredients to make jelly rolls, and cracked seed for his sister Tokie.

Tokie is now 62 and retired recently from the Catholic orphanage in Hiroshima.

Robert Fujiwara, *left,* in 1987 with his wife, Harumi, *center,* on his first visit to Hawaii in forty-nine years, enjoying a reunion with his brothers and their wives. Harry and Bessie are next to him; Hiromi and Ann are at *right. Fujiwara Photo Collection.*

Mrs. Chieno Fujiwara, their mother, died in Hiroshima in 1967 at age 67.

Hiromi and Harry are now retired. Hiromi and his wife, Ann, have three children. Harry and his wife, Bessie, also have three children.

# Chapter 7

# THE YAMAMOTO STORY

It was a chilly November night in Hiroshima City in 1966. But Kazuyuki Yamamoto, 71, kept saying, "*Atatakai* [It's warm]." His crisp, white handkerchief turned limp as he mopped the beads of perspiration from his face. It was perspiration born of his mind's effort to relive what his heart desperately wanted to forget: The A-bomb . . . the death of his wife . . . the death of his daughter.

For two hours that chilly Hiroshima night, Yamamoto sat in a straight-backed chair as he poured out remembrances that were long sealed within himself. He began: "I was born here in Hiroshima. I went to Hawaii in 1919 at the age of 24 as a Japanese language school teacher. Later, I became a principal.

"I taught in Wailuku, Maui, for two years, and then went to the Waianae Japanese School before ending up at the Honolulu Fort Street Gakuen [school]. Twenty-seven years in all. And then December 7, 1941 . . . *yume nimo omowa nakatta* [I never even dreamed it could happen].

"My wife and three daughters, who were born in Hawaii, were in Hiroshima to take care of my sick mother . . . Worry. Yes. Worry. Yes. Worry. But what could I do?

"With many of my friends, I was taken to the internment camps—Tule Lake, Crystal City, and then Santa Fe. It was a long war. But we were treated well. Very well.

"When the war ended, camp officials told us Japan had surrendered. The internees were of two minds. There were those who believed the camp officials, and there were those who

115

didn't. I was in the second group. I thought what the camp officials said about Japan surrendering was all a lie.

"We were given a choice of either returning to Hawaii or going to Japan. I wanted to go to Japan because my family was there. And I was sure Japan had won. On the train en route to our ship in Seattle, I remember one of the guards told us ever so kindly: 'Japan did lose. That's the truth. You can change your mind and stay in the United States. You can change your mind anytime before that ship leaves.' We thought he was lying. I think of that guard even today. My, he was sincere.

"On the boat, we were still in good spirits. Jubilant. We talked about Japan's victory. About a week at sea—a day or so before we reached Japan—one of the Japanese diplomatic officials called the group together. Solemnly, he told us there was no call for rejoicing; Japan had lost the war. We—about five hundred of us—ridiculed him right off the stage.

"We reached Uraga, near Yokosuka, on Christmas Day, 1945. We expected a feast. A huge homecoming feast. Our first shock was when we saw all the shattered glass and bombed-out buildings the moment we got off the ship. There was no feast. Instead, we were fed a horrible broth, unfit for human consumption.

"All of a sudden, we all became quiet. We knew now what the truth was. The officials at the camp had not lied. The guard on the train had not lied. The diplomat on the ship had not lied. The sight and odor of defeat became even stronger on the train ride to Hiroshima City. It took twenty hours. The train was packed tight. No one could move, even to go to the toilet. If you wanted to urinate, you urinated right where you were on the train.

"And then Hiroshima . . . *Bikkuri shimashita* [I was astonished]. The city was flattened out like a field. I rushed to the family home in Kaminagare, Kawa-machi. The house was gone. *Mune ippai* [Heavy, heavy heart] . . . *kuchi de yuwarenai* [I can't describe in words].

A scene of devastation awaited Kazuyuki Yamamoto when he arrived in Hiroshima City at the end of 1945. *Hiroshima Peace Memorial Museum Photo.*

"I walked on to my uncle's in Koi, a suburb. There, I was told that my wife had died in September, a few weeks after the bombing, and my middle daughter had died a month after her. For nearly a year, I wouldn't believe they were dead.

"I learned later that the house was in the heart of the bombing. My wife was pinned under a beam and was fully exposed to the radiation. My older daughter, a teacher's helper, had left the house early—before the bombing—with my youngest daughter, a student. That was so fortunate. So fortunate. But the middle daughter—she was getting ready to go to work at a bank when the bomb fell. A friend told me later that my daughter had seen her mother suffer and then die. So when my daughter's hair began to fall out—when her gums began to bleed—when the diarrhea set in—when she began to get weaker and weaker—she knew that she too was going to die.

"My heart . . . my heart. So very heavy.

"I felt bitter toward the United States, but the bitterness faded. Even then, I thought how well I had been treated in the United States. I thought it was wrong for America to drop such a bomb in such a way. But, too, I thought there must be something wrong with Japan for America to have to drop the bomb. My feelings were complex. *Furafura shite imashita* [I was lost].

"With my oldest and youngest daughters, I built a small home out of the rubble. For two years, I had no spirit to work. *Burabura shite imashita* [I just had no fight in me]. Gradually, I pulled myself together. I locked up my sorrows. Best to forget."

Yamamoto placed his soggy handkerchief into his pocket. His face, which had earlier looked taut and alive, now sagged. Spent. He took a long drink of water from his glass and readily emptied another glassful. And then he said: "We have a group here called the Hiroshima-Hawaii Kai [club]. I'm the president. Sixty of our members get Social Security pensions from the American government. You can live quite well with that here.

"Even now, those of us who were in internment camps talk about the good treatment we had during the war. We've always felt that one of us should put all of that in writing before we die. The wonderful treatment. The bigness of Americans. There's no comparison between the way we were treated and the way prisoners in Japan were mistreated. We always had more than enough to eat. The prisoners here didn't.

"I remember when we first got to the camps, we couldn't have knives and razors. I couldn't understand why at that time. Later, I wondered whether they were trying to protect those who were so depressed from committing suicide.

"I also remember how the camps were always next to U.S. Army camps. At that time, I felt, 'Darn, why should we live next to the soldiers.' Now, I wonder whether that was also for our protection. There was a lot of hysteria in those days. The soldiers may have been there to protect us from the wild ones. Yes, one of us should put all that in writing before we die.

"The Japanese are grateful to the United States for the guidance and help in rebuilding Japan. That's not just a lot of

Kazuyuki Yamamoto in Hiroshima City in 1966. *Author's photo collection.*

empty words. It's the true feeling of the people. I lost a lot in the bombing of Hiroshima, but in the moments when I dare to reflect, I think, perhaps, the bombing was a blessing in disguise. Hiroshima today is a world symbol of peace. That was made possible only because of the bombing."

Yamamoto operates a motor and radio retail outlet and an electroplating plant. His two daughters, who retained their U.S. citizenship, are now married. One of them lives in Los Angeles and the other in Japan.

Yamamoto, too, was remarried a while back, to his younger brother's widow. He said, "She had three children. Relatives suggested that we get together to help each other out. One of the boys is now second in charge of our plant. They're all happily married now."

Yamamoto had 101 questions to ask about Hawaii. He leaned forward as if to confide: "I'd like to go back to Hawaii someday. I'm too old to go there to live. I'd like to visit and play and meet with old friends and students."

The smile that laced his wishful thought stopped short as he pulled himself erect and said: "There's one thing that has always bothered me—like a gnawing pain in my chest. I guess there are those who thought that we Japanese teachers had taught our students to be Japanese, to hate Americans. Many of the nisei boys of the famous 442nd Regimental Combat Team and the 100th Battalion, and many of those who served America so well as Japanese interpreters and translators in the war against Japan were my pupils. They are living proof of what we had always stressed to our students—be good American citizens.

"I'd like that to be known. I'd like that to be printed, just in case anyone still harbors any doubts. I'd like that to be made clear. It has always bothered me."

---■---

## 1990 Update

Kazuyuki Yamamoto died in Hiroshima in 1973 at age 78. He was planning a visit to Hawaii when he became ill. Word of his death was reported by his daughter, Ritsuko Yamamoto Okada, 66, of Yamaguchi Prefecture on a recent trip to Hawaii with her husband, Masanobu Okada. They were both born in Honolulu.

Yamamoto is survived also by his daughter, Hazel Suzuko Sorita, 63, who lives with her husband in Los Angeles. They have two children.

Ritsuko and her husband were both attending separate colleges near the center of the Hiroshima City when the A-bomb exploded. They escaped serious injury, which baffles them. They have three healthy children, which further baffles them.

"We were very, very lucky," Ritsuko said.

# Epilogue

The stories of *Our House Divided*
tell us—
However bitter
the war
their countries wage,
what matters above all
is Brother to Brother  . . .
Love for each other
remains Undivided.

# Acknowledgments

I am happy to come to the end of this book because I can finally thank the many people who helped me technically and personally through my long journey: Mason Altiery, Mona Altiery, Timmie Beam, Les Biller, Lee Ann Bowman, the late Pierre Bowman, Merle and Clara Boyer, Stuart G. Brown, the late Buck Buchwach, Tom Coffman, Phil Damon, Roy and Betsey Essoyan, Renée Finnessy, Sally Fletcher-Murchison, Jocelyn Fujii, June Fukuda, Fred I. Gilbert, Jr., Helen Gilbert, Richard D. Helling, Shurei Hirozawa, my Ala Moana and Kaimana beach friends, Don Horio, Lena Jacobs, Roderick Jacobs, Suzanne Jacobs, Marilyn Kim, Jean S. King, Edward R. Lebb, and the librarians at the Hawaii Newspaper Agency, Manoa, Sinclair, and Hamilton libraries.

Thanks also to Fumi Lopez, Kathy Matsueda, the late Senator Spark Matsunaga, J. J. McNamara, Aldyth Morris and the spirit of Father Damien she keeps alive, Lyle Nelson, my Pahoa classmates and neighbors, Inez Kong Pai, Linus C. Pauling, Jr., Isabelle Perreira, Barry V. Rolett, Tadashi Sato, Fritz Seifert, Marianne Seifert, Harold Smith, John J. Stephan, Charles W. Totto, Roger Whitlock, and Margaret Chinen Yamate.

To the individuals who shared their stories, their lives, with us, my special thanks, and to Iris Wiley and the staff at the University of Hawaii Press, my deepest gratitude.

I assume full responsibility for all errors of fact, style, or inference.

# Additional Reading

Allen, Gwenfread. *Hawaii's War Years 1941–1945*. Honolulu: University of Hawaii Press, 1950.

Coffman, Tom. *Catch a Wave: A Case Study of Hawaii's New Politics*. Honolulu: University of Hawaii Press, 1973.

Daws, Gavan. *Shoal of Time: A History of the Hawaiian Islands*. New York: Macmillan, 1968.

Fuchs, Lawrence H. *Hawaii Pono*. New York: Harcourt Brace, 1961.

Houston, Jeanne Wakatsuki, and James D. Houston. *Farewell to Manzanar*. Boston: Houghton Mifflin, 1973.

Klass, Tim. *World War II on Kauai*. Portland, Ore.: Westland Foundation, 1970.

Lind, Andrew W. *Hawaii's Japanese*. Princeton: Princeton University Press, 1946.

Nordyke, Eleanor C. *The Peopling of Hawai'i*. 2nd ed. Honolulu: University of Hawaii Press, 1989.

Odo, Franklin, and Kazuko Sinoto. *A Pictorial History of the Japanese in Hawai'i, 1885–1924*. Honolulu: Bishop Museum Press, 1985.

Petersen, William. *Japanese Americans: Oppression and Success*. New York: Random House, 1971.

Schmitt, Robert C. *Historical Statistics of Hawaii*. Honolulu: The University Press of Hawaii, 1977.

Stephan, John J. *Hawaii under the Rising Sun: Japan's Plans for Conquest after Pearl Harbor*. Honolulu: University of Hawaii Press, 1984.

Tanaka, Chester. *Go for Broke.* Richmond, Calif.: Go for Broke, Inc., 1982.

Tasaki, Hanama. *Long the Imperial Way.* Boston: Houghton Mifflin, 1950.

U.S. Congress. Commission on Wartime Relocation and Internment of Civilians. *Personal Justice Denied.* Washington: U.S. Government Printing Office, 1982.

# About the Author

Tomi Kaizawa Knaefler was born in the sugar plantation village of Pahoa, Hawaii, in 1929. She began her newspaper career while attending the University of Hawaii as a student columnist and summer reporter for the *Honolulu Advertiser.* She joined the *Honolulu Star-Bulletin* in 1952 and was a staff reporter for twenty-five years. She has won more than a dozen writing honors, including prizes for her news and feature stories from the Honolulu Press Club and awards for her medical writing from the Hawaii Medical Association, American Cancer Society, and the American Psychological Association. She has contributed to two books, but this is her first solo. She enjoys starting each day with an ocean swim and ending each week doing pottery, painting, sewing, or indulgent cooking. Her favorite joy is being a grandmother to Ren and Taylor James.

**Production Notes**

This book was designed by Paula Newcomb. Composition and paging were done on the Quadex Composing System and typesetting on the Compugraphic 8400 by the design and production staff of University of Hawaii Press.

The text typeface is Sabon and the display typeface is Eras.

Offset presswork and binding were done by The Maple-Vail Book Manufacturing Group. Text paper is Glatfelter Offset Vellum, basis 50.